Paula Deen's

2 0 0 8

Calendar

...

Paula

Paula Deen's

2008

Calendar

...

A hearty helping of eye-catchin' pictures,
mouthwaterin' recipes, tantalizin' tips, and
plenty of good ol' Southern charm

RANDOM HOUSE

NEW YORK

Copyright © 2007 by Paula Deen Enterprises, LLC

All rights reserved.

Published in the United States by RANDOM HOUSE,
an imprint of The Random House Publishing Group,
a division of Random House, Inc., New York.

Photograph credits can be found on page 137.

RANDOM HOUSE and colophon
are trademarks of Random House, Inc.

ISBN 978-0-8129-7807-0

LIBRARY OF CONGRESS
CATALOGING-IN-PUBLICATION DATA

Deen, Paula H.

Paula Deen's 2008 calendar.

p. c.m.

ISBN 978-0-8129-7807-0

1. Cookery, American—Southern style.

2. Menus. 3. Holiday cookery. I. Title.

TX715.2.S68D478 2007

641.5975—dc22 2007002670

Printed in the United States of America
on acid-free paper

www.atrandom.com

2 4 6 8 9 7 5 3 1

FIRST EDITION

Calendar design by Barbara M. Bachman

Paula Deen's

2 0 0 8

Calendar

...

*H*appy New Year, y'all! Here we are, at the start of a whole new year, and I'm so glad you're joining me in 2008, as we fill up this calendar with all kinds of delicious things. Now, I cannot let New Year's Day pass without my family consuming black-eyed peas, collard or turnip greens, and hog jowl. (My Granddaddy Paul's superstitions obviously made a big impression on me.) Black-eyed peas were for luck, the greens represented financial success, and the hog jowl was for health, believe it or not. When black-eyed peas and rice are served together, we call it Hoppin' John, and it is pure Southern tradition. But it doesn't matter how you get your black-eyed peas on New Year's Day—just make sure they are consumed in some form or fashion, please.

Sunday	Monday	Tuesday	Wednesday	Thursday	Friday	Saturday
		1	2	3	4	5
6	7	8	9	10	11	12
13	14	15	16	17	18	19
20	21	22	23	24	25	26
27	28	29	30	31		

January

Black-Eyed Peas (FOR GOOD LUCK)
with Hog Jowl (FOR HEALTH)

Black-eyed peas are delicious served with the juices from the pot spooned over white rice, with minced green pepper as a garnish. Most Southerners like to serve their peas with pepper sauce—vinegar mixed with hot peppers—a condiment found in the pickle aisle.

Serves 6 to 8

1 pound dried black-eyed peas
½ pound smoked meat—hog jowl,
 meaty ham hocks, smoked neck
 bones, or smoked ham
1 teaspoon salt

½ teaspoon pepper
4 tablespoons (½ stick) butter
½ cup finely chopped green bell
 pepper, for garnish (optional)
Pepper sauce, for seasoning at the table

1. In a large bowl, cover the peas with water and soak for 1 hour. Drain and discard the soaking water.
2. Place the meat in a 2-quart saucepan and add 2½ cups water. Bring the water to a boil, then reduce the heat to medium low. Cover the pot and cook for 30 minutes. Add the salt and pepper and the peas to the meat and cook until the peas are soft and the liquid has thickened, about 45 minutes. Add the butter and serve. Garnish with green pepper, if desired. Serve with pepper sauce.

TO MAKE HOPPIN' JOHN: Sauté 1 chopped onion, 1 chopped green bell pepper, and 2 minced garlic cloves in 1 tablespoon vegetable oil until soft. Add 2 cups cooked black-eyed peas and 2 cups cooked white rice.

MONDAY, DECEMBER 31

TUESDAY, JANUARY 1

Serve black-eyed peas for good luck,
greens for financial success, hog jowl for health . . .
and let the boys watch their football!

New Year's Day

WEDNESDAY, JANUARY 2

Take some time to recuperate from all the festivities

THURSDAY, JANUARY 3

FRIDAY, JANUARY 4

Plan a fix-it-and-forget-it meal for this weekend,
build yourself a fire, and put your feet up

SATURDAY, JANUARY 5

SUNDAY, JANUARY 6

MONDAY, JANUARY 7

TUESDAY, JANUARY 8

The Lady & Sons opened 12 years ago today!
Elvis's birthday

WEDNESDAY, JANUARY 9

THURSDAY, JANUARY 10

FRIDAY, JANUARY 11

Dust off your Elvis albums, have a few friends over,
and dedicate a meal to the King

SATURDAY, JANUARY 12

Officially time to take down those
Christmas decorations!

SUNDAY, JANUARY 13

*T*he Lady & Sons restaurant had its humble beginnings
back in June 1989 when I started The Bag Lady, a lunch-
delivery service, with my boys, Jamie and Bobby, delivering
bag lunches to area businesspeople in their offices around
Savannah. The Bag Lady expanded in 1991 into a full-service
restaurant named The Lady, located in the Best Western
Hotel on Savannah's Southside. Eventually, I wanted a new
home for The Lady, one in which the ambience matched the
style of food. I found the perfect place in the old Sears,
Roebuck downtown on Congress Street and agreed to a long-
term lease on just a handshake and a smile. After nearly eight
months of renovations and being overdrawn on both bank
accounts, The Lady & Sons opened its doors on January 8,
1996, which was, fittingly, Elvis Presley's birthday! Elvis's
roots ran very deep when it came to the love of his family, and
no matter where he roamed, he knew that there was no place
like home . . . and nothing like home cooking! So it's probably
no coincidence that The Lady & Sons opened on the King's
birthday, and that one of the most popular items on our menu
is a dish that he would have surely loved: Peanut Butter
Gooey Butter Cakes!

Since my recent marriage, my family has doubled in size, and so has the number of birthdays. So, I decided to pick one Sunday in each month and celebrate all the birthdays in that month on that day. One of my rules is "Everybody has his own cake." For this, I confess I head straight to the bakery department and order each guest of honor a personalized cake, but I also bake a homemade pound cake and serve it along with berries, ice cream, and fresh cream. Another rule is that if you're physically able, you must play birthday games, or no cake for you! Everyone works up quite an appetite, so I always plan a meal that is easy to prepare in large quantity.

A few years back, I realized that our childhoods were getting further and further behind us, and that made me sad. So, I set out to find a way to recapture a small piece of that time when our lives were worry-free. I decided to bring back the wonderful, silly games we all played at our birthday celebrations. Well, needless to say, when I announced that the next birthday celebration was going to include games, the moans and groans commenced and my grown-up children said, "But we don't want to play games." Well, once Birthday Sunday came, it took all of about three minutes for the hoots and hollers of laughter to begin. So I'm happy to say, now on Birthday Sundays, when I clap my hands and yell, "Okay, let the games begin!" everybody is eager to play!

MONDAY, JANUARY 14

National Dress 'Up Your Pet Day:
If you can't dress them up, just give them a bath!

TUESDAY, JANUARY 15

WEDNESDAY, JANUARY 16

THURSDAY, JANUARY 17

FRIDAY, JANUARY 18

SATURDAY, JANUARY 19

Paula's birthday (and guess what: she's only 21!)

SUNDAY, JANUARY 20

Birthday Sunday: All January birthdays celebrate today!

MONDAY, JANUARY 21

Seed catalogs begin to arrive; start making those lists!

TUESDAY, JANUARY 22

WEDNESDAY, JANUARY 23

Today is National Pie Day!

THURSDAY, JANUARY 24

FRIDAY, JANUARY 25

If you live in a snowy area, de-ice those
windows and pull those icicles off your gutters!

SATURDAY, JANUARY 26

SUNDAY, JANUARY 27

Beer-in-the-Rear Chicken

Succulent and delicious, this hilarious-looking way to grill chicken is perfect for big, fun parties like Birthday Sundays, since it's virtually self-basting.

1 chicken serves 2 to 4, depending on appetites
(my crowd can eat half a chicken each, easy!)

1 chicken (3 pounds)
Seasoned salt
House Seasoning (recipe is at the
*   end of this calendar)*

One 12-ounce can beer
1 sprig rosemary
Assorted barbecue and hot sauces,
*   your choice*

1. Wash and drain the chicken and pat dry. Coat the chicken inside and out with seasoned salt and House Seasoning. Refrigerate until ready to cook.

2. Prepare the charcoal grill. (You can use a gas grill, but I love the taste you get with charcoal!) When the coals are hot and glowing, carefully push them over to the sides of the grill, leaving an open space in the middle.

3. Open the can of beer and pour off approximately ¼ cup. Insert the sprig of rosemary into the can, then place the can, upright, into the rear cavity of the chicken. Carefully stand the chicken up on the beer can, and place it in the center of the grill, facing one of the banks of coals, making sure not to spill the beer. Cover the grill and cook the chicken for approximately 1 hour, or until done, rotating as necessary. The chicken is done when the juice runs clear when pierced with a fork.

4. Carefully remove the beer can from the chicken using oven mitts, and discard the can. Cut the chicken into halves or quarters. I personally don't want any sauce on this chicken, but I always offer barbecue sauces and hot sauces to my guests.

* Seasoned salt is table salt flavored with herbs, spices, and other flavorings (and sometimes MSG). It's available in supermarkets.

February always reminds me of one of my favorite holidays—Valentine's Day. I like to think of it as a night for lovers, and it's the one day at The Lady & Sons that we take reservations for tables for two. At home, Michael's job is to make sure I have a big bouquet of flowers, and my job is to make him a delicious meal. Some of his favorite foods are shrimp, lobster, steak, and chocolate, so I'll make my version of surf-'n'-turf and something rich and decadent for dessert. This Valentine's Day, I'll probably set us a beautifully laid table in our private garden and have a fireplace going—real romantic and intimate.

Sunday	Monday	Tuesday	Wednesday	Thursday	Friday	Saturday
					1	2
3	4	5	6	7	8	9
10	11	12	13	14	15	16
17	18	19	20	21	22	23
24	25	26	27	28	29	

February

MONDAY, JANUARY 28

Visit the market and take advantage of all
the wonderful winter vegetables filling the aisles;
stock up for pies, soups, and stews

TUESDAY, JANUARY 29

WEDNESDAY, JANUARY 30

THURSDAY, JANUARY 31

Make way for February, a big birthday month
in the Groover/Deen household!

FRIDAY, FEBRUARY 1

SATURDAY, FEBRUARY 2

Groundhog Day. How many more days
of winter will we have?

SUNDAY, FEBRUARY 3

Get ready for Fat Tuesday—Mardi Gras!

Breakfast Casserole

When it's cold outside, I like to make up a big hearty breakfast, and this casserole is a great way to warm up the whole family. Preheat the oven, pop it in, and the house will wake up to the smell of something yummy. As a matter of fact, you have to make this savory casserole the night before you eat it so the bread soaks up all the seasoned egg mixture, so it's always one less thing to worry about in the morning.

Serves 6 to 8

5 slices thick-sliced white bread, crust
    and all, buttered and cubed
1 pound mild sausage, cooked,
    crumbled, and drained
3 cups grated extra-sharp Cheddar
    cheese

4 eggs
2 cups milk
1 teaspoon dry mustard
1 teaspoon salt
1 teaspoon hot sauce

1. Spray a 1½-quart casserole dish with vegetable-oil cooking spray. Place the bread cubes in the casserole. Evenly distribute the sausage over the bread cubes. Sprinkle evenly with the cheese. Combine the eggs, milk, mustard, salt, and hot sauce, and mix well. Pour the egg mixture over the bread. Cover with plastic wrap and refrigerate overnight.

2. The next morning, remove the casserole from the refrigerator and allow it to sit on the counter for 15 minutes while you preheat the oven to 350°F. Remove the plastic wrap, place the casserole in the oven, and bake for 1 hour.

Jambalaya

This is it: the granddaddy of New Orleans tradition! With chicken, sausage, shrimp, oysters, and crab in it, how could this be anything but good?

Serves 6 to 8 as a main course, 10 to 12 as part of a buffet

1 teaspoon salt
2 large chicken breast halves,
   on the bone
1 1/2 tablespoons butter
2 cloves garlic, minced
1 cup chopped celery
1 cup chopped green bell pepper
1/2 cup chopped yellow onion
2 cups cooked white rice
1 pound smoked sausage, such as
   kielbasa, cut into 1-inch pieces

One 14.5-ounce can Creole-spiced
   stewed tomatoes
1/2 cup dry sherry
1 1/2 pounds medium raw shrimp,
   peeled and deveined
1 cup shucked raw oysters, drained
1 cup (8 ounces) fresh crabmeat, picked
   through twice for shells
Salt and pepper
Hot sauce (optional)

1. In a 3-quart saucepan with a lid, place 2 cups water and the salt. Bring the water to a boil, reduce the heat, and gently boil the chicken breasts until done, about 25 minutes. Allow the breasts to cool in the broth, then remove them, reserving the broth. Shred the chicken meat and set aside.

2. In a small sauté pan, melt the butter. Sauté the garlic, celery, green pepper, and onion until limp, about 3 minutes. Set aside.

3. In the original 3-quart saucepan, bring the chicken broth to a boil. Add the rice and sausage. Bring back to a boil. Add the tomatoes, sautéed vegetables, shredded chicken, and sherry. Simmer for about 15 minutes.

4. Add the shrimp, oysters, and crabmeat. Cover and cook until the shrimp are pink, 5 to 8 minutes.

5. Check for seasoning and add salt and pepper to taste. Add hot sauce, if desired.

MONDAY, FEBRUARY 4

TUESDAY, FEBRUARY 5

It's Mardi Gras—let the good times roll!
Or as they say down in New Orleans, laissez
les bon temps rouler!

WEDNESDAY, FEBRUARY 6

THURSDAY, FEBRUARY 7

Review those seed catalogs and place your order for spring

FRIDAY, FEBRUARY 8

SATURDAY, FEBRUARY 9

SUNDAY, FEBRUARY 10

$\mathcal{V}$alentine's Day, one of my favorite holidays, always gets me thinking of my sweetie, Michael. One of my favorite stories about our courtship was our very first kiss. As everyone knows, Michael has a rather long beard. At the end of our first date, just when I was thinking about kissing him, I started worrying about the beard. I said, "I have never kissed a man with a beard!" And he joked right back, "Neither have I." So after a good laugh Michael leaned in for the kiss, but instead of kissing him back, I grabbed his upper lip, wantin' to find out just what was under all that beard! Well, I was relieved and delighted to find he had a full set of clean white teeth!! Y'all know that kiss was not a problem, but him not having teeth could have been a big one!

MONDAY, FEBRUARY 11

Start making plans for Valentine's Day!

TUESDAY, FEBRUARY 12

WEDNESDAY, FEBRUARY 13

THURSDAY, FEBRUARY 14

Valentine's Day... spend it with your honey!

FRIDAY, FEBRUARY 15

SATURDAY, FEBRUARY 16

SUNDAY, FEBRUARY 17

MONDAY, FEBRUARY 18

Presidents' Day

TUESDAY, FEBRUARY 19

WEDNESDAY, FEBRUARY 20

THURSDAY, FEBRUARY 21

FRIDAY, FEBRUARY 22

SATURDAY, FEBRUARY 23

SUNDAY, FEBRUARY 24

Birthday Sunday

Strawberry Cheese Ring

In January 2006, my crew went to Plains, Georgia, to film one of my shows right in Mr. Jimmy Carter's own kitchen! Like me, he likes traditional Southern food, and I've heard this was his favorite cheese dish. Mr. Jimmy's First Lady, Rosalynn Carter, has been credited for making this a famous Southern favorite.

Serves approximately 20

16 ounces sharp Cheddar cheese, grated
One 3-ounce package cream cheese, softened
3/4 cup mayonnaise
1 small onion, chopped

1 cup chopped pecans or walnuts
1/2 teaspoon garlic salt or powder
Cayenne pepper to taste
1 cup strawberry preserves

1. Combine all ingredients except the preserves in a food processor or electric mixer. Mix thoroughly and refrigerate for 2 to 3 hours. Scoop the mixture onto a platter.

2. Use your hands to mold the mixture into a ring formation (I suggest placing a sheet of wax paper between your hands and the mixture to prevent melting and stickiness). Spread the strawberry preserves in the center of the ring, and serve with some good buttery crackers.

My handsome baby brother, Bubba, means so much to me and was such an enormous help when I was starting up my first restaurant, The Lady & Sons. So you can bet that I couldn't wait to return the favor! A few years back, at Christmastime 2004, he and I opened up a new restaurant in Savannah on Whitemarsh Island, called Uncle Bubba's Oyster House. You'll just have to come down and try his char-grilled oysters, the specialty of the house. The food's so good it will make you slap your mama! And you'll just love the view. We're right on Turner's Creek. And rest assured, our Aunt Peggy was there for the opening, making sure everything was just so.

MONDAY, FEBRUARY 25

Make something fun and colorful to cheer up yourself
and your loved ones during the February weather

TUESDAY, FEBRUARY 26

WEDNESDAY, FEBRUARY 27

My stepson Michael Anthony Groover, Jr.'s birthday

THURSDAY, FEBRUARY 28

My baby brother Bubba's birthday!

FRIDAY, FEBRUARY 29

It's a leap year!

SATURDAY, MARCH 1

Shop for Michael's anniversary gift

SUNDAY, MARCH 2

The first week of March, a very special, truly romantic week, always keeps me and Michael very busy 'cause our anniversary falls on the sixth (and not to be outdone, my son Jamie and his wife, Brooke, celebrate theirs on the fifth). Our wedding reception was held at The Lady & Sons, and everyone dined on shrimp and grits, miniature crab cakes, collard green wontons, mini handle sandwiches, and other decadent Southern fare. I think I speak for both of us when I say our lives are finally complete. Here's a thought I'd like to share with y'all: If it can happen to me, it can happen to you.

Sunday	Monday	Tuesday	Wednesday	Thursday	Friday	Saturday
						1
2	3	4	5	6	7	8
9	10	11	12	13	14	15
16	17	18	19	20	21	22
23	24	25	26	27	28	29
30	31					

March

MONDAY, MARCH 3

TUESDAY, MARCH 4

WEDNESDAY, MARCH 5

Prepare Michael's favorite Banana Nut Cake

Jamie and Brooke's anniversary

THURSDAY, MARCH 6

Wish my honey a happy fourth anniversary!

My niece Corrie's birthday!

FRIDAY, MARCH 7

SATURDAY, MARCH 8

SUNDAY, MARCH 9

Daylight Savings Time begins

Banana Nut Cake

Hands down, this is Michael's favorite cake. It's a sweet, scrumptious memory of the days when his mother, Carmel, would bake it for him. So naturally, this just had to be his groom's cake!

Serves 18 to 20

CAKE

Butter, for greasing pans
3 cups all-purpose flour, plus more for
    dusting pans
2 cups sugar
1 teaspoon baking soda
1 teaspoon ground cinnamon
1/2 teaspoon salt
3 eggs, beaten
3/4 cup vegetable oil
4 large ripe bananas, mashed

1 cup chopped pecans
1 1/2 teaspoons vanilla extract

FROSTING

8 ounces cream cheese, at room
    temperature
1/2 cup (1 stick) butter, at room
    temperature
1 pound confectioners' sugar, sifted
1 teaspoon vanilla extract
1/2 cup chopped pecans

1. Butter and flour three 9-inch round cake pans; set aside. Preheat oven to 350°F.

2. In a mixing bowl, stir together the flour, sugar, baking soda, cinnamon, and salt. Add the eggs and oil and stir just until the dry ingredients are moistened; do not beat. Stir in the bananas, pecans, and vanilla. Divide the batter among the prepared pans and bake for 23 to 28 minutes, or until a wooden pick inserted in the center comes out clean. Cool the cake layers in the pans for 10 minutes, then turn them out onto a rack to cool completely. While the cake cools, make the frosting.

3. In a bowl, blend together the cream cheese and butter. Gradually add the confectioners' sugar and beat until light and fluffy. Beat in the vanilla. Stir in the pecans, or reserve them to sprinkle over the frosted cake. Fill and frost the cake when it is completely cool.

Note: If you are interested in using this recipe for a wedding cake, consult a professional baker, as quantities and bake time will vary based on the number of people you plan to feed.

Y'all know that baking is one of my favorite things to do, and I'm happy to share so many of my favorite dessert recipes. Here are a few hints I've picked up over the years:

* Most recipe instructions call for greased and floured pans. I use a fat-free cooking spray like Pam or Baker's Joy. If you don't use those, grease your pan with solid shortening instead of oil.

* Try to avoid opening the oven door to peek until the minimum cooking time is up.

* If a recipe calls for "X cups of sifted flour," that means to sift the flour before measuring. If it calls for "X cups of flour, sifted," sift the flour after measuring.

* Adding a pinch of salt to the sugar when making icing will prevent graining.

* To "fix" an overbaked cake, make a simple syrup of equal parts water and sugar along with a teaspoonful of flavoring (lemon, vanilla, maple, etc.) or a teaspoonful or two of a liqueur (or rum or brandy). Bring to a boil, remove from the heat, and allow to cool. Pierce cake layers with a fork and brush each with the amount of syrup you think it needs. If this doesn't correct the texture, don't despair—cut the cake up into pieces and use in a trifle recipe.

MONDAY, MARCH 10

TUESDAY, MARCH 11

WEDNESDAY, MARCH 12

THURSDAY, MARCH 13

Place order for Easter ham

FRIDAY, MARCH 14

SATURDAY, MARCH 15

SUNDAY, MARCH 16

Birthday Sunday!

Palm Sunday

MONDAY, MARCH 17

St. Patrick's Day

TUESDAY, MARCH 18

WEDNESDAY, MARCH 19

Make sure you have enough platters for Easter supper

THURSDAY, MARCH 20

FRIDAY, MARCH 21

Good Friday

SATURDAY, MARCH 22

Hide those Easter eggs for the little ones!

SUNDAY, MARCH 23

Easter Sunday

Peanut Butter-Glazed Ham

When I was growing up, my family's Easter meal always featured ham. This delicious meat goes well with any number of glazes, but this one is really yummy with the saltiness of the ham. You can use it over grilled ham slices, too.

Serves 12 to 14

One 10-to-12-pound whole smoked
    picnic ham, rinsed and patted dry,
    untrimmed
1 cup chicken broth

$^1/_2$ cup creamy peanut butter
$^1/_4$ cup honey
1 clove garlic, chopped
2 teaspoons soy sauce

1. Position an oven rack in the lower third of your oven. Preheat the oven to 325°F.

2. Place the ham on a rack in a roasting pan. Place the pan in the oven and roast the ham for 20 minutes per pound. If the ham begins to burn, cover loosely with foil.

3. At the end of the cooking time, in a blender or a food processor, combine the broth, peanut butter, honey, garlic, and soy sauce. Slather the glaze all over the surface of the ham and cook for an additional 20 minutes.

4. Remove the ham from the oven and allow it to sit for about 15 minutes before carving.

Way back in the mid-1990s, I received a call from Martha Nesbit, who was the food editor of the Savannah Morning News. *She wanted the recipe for my son Jamie's chicken salad, one of our popular menu items, and I was thrilled to pieces to share it with her. We've been friends ever since, and let me tell you, that girl can cook! Years later, Bobby Flay made a point to tell me that, hands down, Martha's shrimp and grits were the best he'd ever tasted!*

Martha's Shrimp and Grits

Here it is, y'all, my good friend Martha Nesbit's beloved shrimp and grits recipe. This is comfort food at its finest, and can even be dressed up by serving it in a tall martini glass or a gold-rimmed soup plate; it's all in the presentation, and it is simply perfect for a Good Friday supper.

Serves 8 as an appetizer or 4 as a main course

1 cup stone-ground grits
Salt and pepper
¼ cup (½ stick) butter
2 cups shredded sharp Cheddar cheese
1 pound raw shrimp, peeled and deveined, left whole if small and roughly chopped if medium or large

6 slices bacon, chopped into tiny pieces
4 teaspoons fresh lemon juice
2 tablespoons chopped fresh parsley
1 cup thinly sliced green onions, white and green parts
1 large clove garlic, minced

1. In a medium saucepan, bring 4 cups water to a boil. Add the grits and salt and pepper to taste. Stir well with a whisk. Reduce the heat to the lowest possible setting and cook the grits until all the water is absorbed, about 10 to 15 minutes. Remove from the heat and stir in the butter and cheese. Keep covered until ready to serve.

2. Rinse the shrimp and pat dry. Fry the bacon in a large skillet until browned and crisp, then drain on a paper towel. Add the shrimp to the bacon grease in the skillet, and sauté over medium heat just until they turn pink, about 3 minutes. Do not overcook! Immediately add the lemon juice, parsley, green onions, and garlic. Remove the skillet from the heat.

3. Pour the grits into a serving bowl. Pour the shrimp mixture over the grits. Garnish with the bacon bits.

4. If you are serving this as an appetizer, spoon ¼ cup grits onto a bread or salad plate. Top with ¼ cup of the shrimp mixture. Garnish with a sprinkling of crisp bacon bits and serve immediately.

MONDAY, MARCH 24

TUESDAY, MARCH 25

WEDNESDAY, MARCH 26

THURSDAY, MARCH 27

FRIDAY, MARCH 28

SATURDAY, MARCH 29

SUNDAY, MARCH 30

In the South, we can dine outdoors for much of the year (okay, so we fight the gnats and the mosquitoes, but we enjoy the outdoors anyway). What's so nice about an outdoor party is that the guests can stand around, chat, and watch and smell the main course cooking. April (assuming it isn't raining) is one of the best times of the year to eat outdoors; it's neither too hot nor too cold, wherever you live.

I happen to like cold accompaniments with my grilled meat. Nothing tastes better, for example, on a warm Southern evening than some peach pickles. I like to make my own with fresh sweet peaches, but if you live where the fresh peaches taste like cardboard, look for peach pickles at the grocery store.

Sunday	Monday	Tuesday	Wednesday	Thursday	Friday	Saturday
		1	2	3	4	5
6	7	8	9	10	11	12
13	14	15	16	17	18	19
20	21	22	23	24	25	26
27	28	29	30			

April

MONDAY, MARCH 31

TUESDAY, APRIL 1

April Fool's Day

WEDNESDAY, APRIL 2

THURSDAY, APRIL 3

Take to the garden! April is National Gardening Month.

FRIDAY, APRIL 4

SATURDAY, APRIL 5

Time for a Saturday night grill party

SUNDAY, APRIL 6

*W*hen planning a Saturday night grill party, by all means, keep it simple. Here are some of my favorite tips for hosting an easy, fun outdoor night:

* Choose plates in bright, summery colors (even if it's still spring)—Fiesta ware comes to mind—and use lots of candles to set the mood.
* A simple bowl of fresh fruit can serve as a beautiful, easy-to-put-together centerpiece.
* Make your appetizers ahead of time, so that you can stand around and sniff with your guests.
* Allow the meat to marinate up to 24 hours if possible.
* Buy grill baskets with nonstick coating for easier cleanup, and spray them with vegetable-oil cooking spray.
* Grilling is a great to way to please everyone. Choose your favorites, or do what I sometimes do—cook a little bit of everything and let your guests have a mixed grill.

Paula's Ultimate Oatmeal Cookies

People may claim to be counting calories and carbs, but who in their right mind will turn down a homemade cookie? You can always find folks willing to chuck their diets to attend a cookie swap! This party makes a nice wedding shower (every new bride needs good cookie recipes to try out on her new husband and neighbors) or baby shower (every mother needs a stash of recipes to take to preschool parties, swim meets, and ballet recitals). I created this recipe on my television show. I could have eaten the whole plateful myself—and I just about did!

Makes about 5 dozen

1/2 cup (1 stick) butter, softened
1/2 cup vegetable shortening
1 1/2 cups packed light brown sugar
2 eggs
1/2 cup buttermilk
1 3/4 cups all-purpose flour
1 teaspoon baking soda
1/2 teaspoon salt
1 teaspoon baking powder
1 teaspoon ground ginger
1 teaspoon freshly grated nutmeg
1 teaspoon ground cinnamon

1/4 teaspoon ground cloves
1/2 teaspoon ground allspice
2 1/2 cups quick-cooking oats
    (not instant!)
1 cup raisins
1 1/2 cups chopped walnuts
1 teaspoon vanilla extract

BROWN BUTTER ICING
1/2 cup (1 stick) butter
3 cups sifted confectioners' sugar
1 teaspoon vanilla extract

1. Preheat the oven to 350°F. Line cookie sheets with parchment paper or nonstick baking mats.
2. Using an electric mixer, cream together the butter, shortening, and sugar at a low speed until fluffy. Add the eggs and beat until the mixture is light in color. Add the buttermilk and mix to combine.
3. Sift together the flour, baking soda, salt, baking powder, ginger, nutmeg, cinnamon, cloves, and allspice. Using a low mixer speed, gradually add the dry ingredients to the butter-egg mixture. With a spatula, fold in the oats, raisins, walnuts, and vanilla, blending well. Drop by rounded teaspoonfuls 1½ inches apart onto the prepared cookie sheets. Bake for 12 to 15 minutes.
4. While the cookies are baking, make the icing. In a small saucepan, heat the butter over medium heat until golden brown, stirring occasionally. Remove the saucepan from the heat; stir in the sugar and vanilla. Stir in enough water (3 to 4 tablespoons) to make an icing of drizzling consistency.
5. Remove the cookies to wire racks to cool. Drizzle with Brown Butter Icing while the cookies are still warm.

MONDAY, APRIL 7

TUESDAY, APRIL 8

WEDNESDAY, APRIL 9

Host a Wednesday-afternoon cookie swap

THURSDAY, APRIL 10

FRIDAY, APRIL 11

SATURDAY, APRIL 12

SUNDAY, APRIL 13

MONDAY, APRIL 14

National Pecan Day

TUESDAY, APRIL 15

Remember to pay your taxes!

WEDNESDAY, APRIL 16

THURSDAY, APRIL 17

FRIDAY, APRIL 18

SATURDAY, APRIL 19

Passover begins at sundown

SUNDAY, APRIL 20

Turtle Pizza

I've always enjoyed curling up in my bed and watching a good movie. I'll admit it: Michael and I love to eat in our bed! And pizza is one of those foods where it never dawns on us to take it to the table, especially not when we're watching movies. It's hard to think about movies without thinking about candy, and here's a "pizza" inspired by the flavors of the traditional turtle, which is often just packed with delicious, sweet pecans.

In the South, pecans are everywhere this time of year, and this is a great way to celebrate April 14—National Pecan Day.

Makes 32 wedges

Four 10-inch flour tortillas
One 12-ounce package caramel
  candies, unwrapped

½ cup sweetened condensed milk
1 cup chocolate chips
1 cup toasted pecan pieces

1. Preheat the oven to 350°F. Cut each tortilla into 8 wedges. Bake the tortilla wedges for 7 to 9 minutes, until a light golden color. (If you try to cut the baked tortilla, it will break and crack.)

2. Combine the caramels and condensed milk in a microwave-safe glass dish. Microwave on high (100%) for 1 minute, stir, and microwave again for 1 minute. Stir again. When the caramels are melted, stir the mixture until smooth. Spread it evenly on the 32 tortilla wedges.

3. Melt the chocolate chips in a microwave-safe glass dish on high (100%) for 1 minute, stir, and microwave 10 seconds more. Stir until smooth. Spread the chocolate layer over the caramel layer. Sprinkle the pecans evenly over the chocolate. Refrigerate until serving time.

MONDAY, APRIL 21

TUESDAY, APRIL 22

Earth Day

WEDNESDAY, APRIL 23

THURSDAY, APRIL 24

FRIDAY, APRIL 25

National Arbor Day . . . get out there and plant a tree!

SATURDAY, APRIL 26

SUNDAY, APRIL 27

Birthday Sunday!

Anyone who knows me knows how much I value hard work. But at the same time, what's the worth of working hard if you can't have a little fun too? Some of my favorite moments have been with my friend Brandon Branch, who's also my executive assistant. One time, my man Michael and I had just gotten new Jet Skis. Brandon had never been on one, so I took him for a ride. I kept steering into the marsh grass, which was, of course, being sucked into the engine. I didn't know what that would do, and Michael said, "Get out of the grass!" Well, I took off at full throttle, almost throwing Brandon into the water. He thought he was going to die, and I was laughin' and havin' a great ol' time. According to Brandon, the moral of the story is to NEVER ride on a Jet Ski with Paula Deen!

The Kentucky Derby is real Southern tradition, and fans who watch the races from home often plan an event centered around mint juleps (the classic Derby drink made with fresh mint, good Kentucky bourbon, and sugar syrup, traditionally served ice-cold in a silver julep cup), the television set, and good food, including what some consider to be Kentucky's finest delicacy: fresh-off-the-farm salt-cured country ham, complete with a moldy exterior. But you don't have to be from Kentucky or serve a country ham to have a bona fide Derby party. My friends Sue and Lou Off, of Tybee Island, Georgia, invite us in for mint juleps, cheese straws, pimiento cheese spread, marinated shrimp, and a lot more.

Sunday	Monday	Tuesday	Wednesday	Thursday	Friday	Saturday
				1	2	3
4	5	6	7	8	9	10
11	12	13	14	15	16	17
18	19	20	21	22	23	24
25	26	27	28	29	30	31

May

Bobby's Goulash

People ask me daily what my favorite meal is, expecting they already know the answer, but they're usually surprised when I say, "The goulash my mama makes for my birthday every year." I have it only once a year, and that's what makes it such a wonderful family tradition.

—Bobby Deen

This dish is basically a glorified Beefaroni! I would describe it as almost a thick spaghetti sauce, chock-full of elbow macaroni and lean ground beef. Delicious!

Serves 6 (unless Bobby's eating—then it serves about 3)

2 pounds lean ground beef
1 pound ground turkey
2 large yellow onions, chopped
Two 15-ounce cans tomato sauce
Two 15-ounce cans diced tomatoes
3 cloves garlic, chopped
2 tablespoons Italian seasoning

3 bay leaves
3 tablespoons soy sauce
1 tablespoon House Seasoning (recipe is at the end of this calendar)
1 tablespoon seasoned salt
2 cups elbow macaroni (uncooked)

1. In a Dutch oven, sauté the ground beef and ground turkey over medium-high heat until no pink remains. Break up the meat while sautéing. Spoon off any grease. Add the onions to the pot and sauté until they are tender, about 5 minutes. Add 3 cups water, along with the tomato sauce, tomatoes, garlic, Italian seasoning, bay leaves, soy sauce, House Seasoning, and seasoned salt. Stir well. Place a lid on the pot and allow this to cook for 15 to 20 minutes.

2. Add the elbow macaroni, stir well, return the lid to the pot, and simmer for about 30 minutes. Turn off the heat, remove the bay leaves, and allow the mixture to sit about 30 minutes before serving.

3. Serve with garlic bread and a salad.

MONDAY, APRIL 28

My boy Bobby's birthday!

TUESDAY, APRIL 29

WEDNESDAY, APRIL 30

THURSDAY, MAY 1

May Day

FRIDAY, MAY 2

SATURDAY, MAY 3

Kentucky Derby Day: the Run for the Roses!
Ladies, put on your fancy hats and
make yourselves a mint julep!

SUNDAY, MAY 4

Cucumber Sandwiches

Afternoon tea is an English tradition, and since Savannah was founded by the English, it is a perfect choice for a Mother's Day celebration. Front and center at tea are always delicious cucumber sandwiches. I like to use thin-skinned English cucumbers (also called hothouse cucumbers) for these because they have fewer seeds and a sweeter flavor than the regular super-market kind. Mix white and pumpernickel breads for variety, if you wish.

Makes about 25 sandwiches

1 English cucumber, at least 8 inches
*   long*
1 cup mayonnaise
6 tablespoons sour cream

1 tablespoon grated yellow onion
½ teaspoon seasoned salt
Two 1-pound loaves thin-sliced bread,
*   white or pumpernickel or 1 of each*

1. Wash the cucumber. Take a fork and score the peel from top to bottom. Trim the ends and slice the cucumber ¼ inch thick; you should have about 25 slices. Place the slices on paper towels to drain.

2. In a small bowl, combine the mayonnaise, sour cream, onion, and seasoned salt. Using a small biscuit cutter or juice glass, cut the bread into rounds the size of the cucumber slices. Spread a bread round with the mayonnaise mixture and place a cucumber on top. Top with a second bread round.

Tip: If you plan your afternoon tea for the Saturday before Mother's Day, you can spend the day with your own family that Sunday. You may want to invite some little girls, too, because probably very few of them have ever been to a real tea.

MONDAY, MAY 5

It's Cinco de Mayo, so get out those piñatas and make yourself a Margarita!

TUESDAY, MAY 6

WEDNESDAY, MAY 7

THURSDAY, MAY 8

FRIDAY, MAY 9

SATURDAY, MAY 10

Have a special Mother's Day tea

SUNDAY, MAY 11

Mother's Day

*N*ow, if there's one thing that May is good for, it's a thorough, head-to-toe spring housecleaning. Whether you're ready to start entertaining and don't want your guests to be staring down a bunch of dust bunnies or you just want a fresh, clean start to the season, here are some helpful hints to get your house in tip-top shape:

* To sanitize cutting boards and countertops, use a mixture of 1 tablespoon bleach to 1 gallon of water.
* To deodorize jars, pour in a solution of 1 tablespoon dry mustard and 1 gallon of warm water. To deodorize plastic containers, wad up newspaper, place it in the containers, cover, and let sit overnight.
* To clean a toilet: Pour a can of Coca-Cola into the toilet bowl. Let the "real thing" sit for 1 hour, then flush clean. The citric acid in Coke removes stains from vitreous china.
* To remove grease from clothes: Empty a can of Coca-Cola into a load of greasy clothes in your washer, add detergent, and run through a regular cycle. The Coke will help loosen grease stains.

MONDAY, MAY 12

TUESDAY, MAY 13

Deadhead the season's first roses

WEDNESDAY, MAY 14

THURSDAY, MAY 15

Send out invitations for a Memorial Day Backyard Bash

FRIDAY, MAY 16

SATURDAY, MAY 17

SUNDAY, MAY 18

Bert's Southern Fried Chicken

You'll need a well-seasoned cast-iron skillet to make this all-American dish that is just perfect for your Memorial Day Backyard Bash!

Serves 4 to 6

*1 chicken (3 pounds), washed and cut
   into 8 serving pieces
Salt and pepper
2 cups all-purpose or self-rising flour*

*3 eggs
1/3 cup milk
Peanut oil for frying*

1. Several hours before cooking, liberally sprinkle each piece of chicken with salt and pepper. Place the chicken in a dish, cover with plastic wrap, and set in the refrigerator.

2. Place the flour in a plastic kitchen storage bag. When ready to cook, beat the eggs with the milk. Dip the chicken pieces into the egg mixture, then place each piece in the bag. Shake until the chicken is coated. Set the floured chicken on a plate while you heat the oil.

3. Pour enough oil into a cast-iron skillet to come only about halfway up the sides. This is important, as the oil rises when each piece of chicken is added. (You must be careful not to let the oil spill out while the chicken is frying; it can cause serious burns or cause a grease fire if it lands on a gas flame or electric cooktop.)

4. Turn the heat to medium high; test by adding a drop of water to the oil. If it sizzles, the oil is ready; this takes about 4 to 5 minutes. Place about 4 pieces of chicken into the hot oil. Allow to cook on the first side about 8 minutes, and on the second about 6 minutes, until brown and crispy. Pieces with large bones—the legs and thighs—may need an additional minute per side to get completely done. Remove the chicken from the oil and drain well on brown paper bags. Cook the second batch of chicken.

5. Wrap the chicken tightly in aluminum foil to keep warm, or place in aluminum pans with parchment paper between layers.

MONDAY, MAY 19

TUESDAY, MAY 20

WEDNESDAY, MAY 21

Create your Memorial Day Backyard Bash checklist

THURSDAY, MAY 22

FRIDAY, MAY 23

SATURDAY, MAY 24

SUNDAY, MAY 25

Have a combination Birthday Sunday
and Memorial Day Backyard Bash!

There's nothing I like better than using fresh, seasonal produce in my cooking, and there's no better time to celebrate the bounty of my garden than the beginning of summer! Here are a few of my very favorite vegetable recipes, perfect for a great big green outdoor bash.

Sweet Potato Chips

Serves 4

2 large sweet potatoes
8 tablespoons (1 stick) butter, melted

1 cup honey-roasted peanuts, chopped
Salt to taste

Preheat the oven to 450°F. Line two large baking sheets with foil; lightly grease. Slice the potatoes ¼ inch thick. Dip in melted butter and arrange on the baking sheets so that the chips do not overlap. Sprinkle with peanuts. Bake for 15 to 20 minutes. Sprinkle with salt.

Fried Green Tomatoes

Serves 6

3 or 4 large, firm green tomatoes
Salt
2 cups self-rising flour or cornmeal

1 to 2 teaspoons pepper
Vegetable oil for frying

Slice the tomatoes to desired thickness (I prefer mine thin). Lay out on a pan and sprinkle with salt. Place in a colander and allow time for the salt to pull the water out of the tomatoes. Mix the flour with the pepper. Coat the tomatoes with the flour mixture, and deep-fry until golden brown.

Creamed Corn

Serves 3 to 4

1 dozen ears fresh corn
8 tablespoons (1 stick) butter

Salt and pepper to taste

Remove the corn from the cob using a corn grater. (If you have to use a knife, cut the tips off the kernels, then, using the blade of the knife, scrape the remaining corn off the cob; this will produce a creamy corn.) Put the corn in a glass dish and put the stick of butter on top. Cook in a microwave oven on high about 7 to 10 minutes, stopping to turn and stir a couple of times. Be careful not to overcook. If the corn seems too dry, add a little milk or water. Season with salt and pepper to taste.

MONDAY, MAY 26

Memorial Day

TUESDAY, MAY 27

My stepdaughter Michelle Groover's birthday!

WEDNESDAY, MAY 28

THURSDAY, MAY 29

FRIDAY, MAY 30

SATURDAY, MAY 31

SUNDAY, JUNE 1

Whether you're celebrating birthdays, graduations, weddings, Father's Day, or just the beginning of summer, Sunday afternoons in June are the perfect time to have casual get-togethers. Shorts, T-shirts, and barbecues are essential for summertime, and at this time of year you'll never have to look for a reason to get together. Just keep things simple and fresh; you can even ask everyone to bring their favorite salad or dessert to make it easy on yourself.

Sunday	Monday	Tuesday	Wednesday	Thursday	Friday	Saturday
1	2	3	4	5	6	7
8	9	10	11	12	13	14
15	15	17	18	19	20	21
22	23	24	25	26	27	28
29	30					

June

The Lady's Coleslaw

No summertime get-together is complete without coleslaw, and this recipe is one of our favorites. To me, the secret to good slaw is the way you cut your cabbage. I have found that I prefer half of the cabbage coarsely chopped in a food processor and half hand-sliced very thin. Use outside dark green leaves, too, for color.

Serves approximately 6

¹/₂ bell pepper, chopped
1 green onion, chopped
¹/₂ large carrot, chopped
¹/₈ cup chopped fresh parsley
¹/₂ head cabbage
¹/₂ cup mayonnaise
2 tablespoons sugar

¹/₂ teaspoon Jane's Krazy Mixed-Up
   Salt
¹/₂ teaspoon coarsely ground black
   pepper
¹/₄ teaspoon lemon-pepper seasoning
1 tablespoon white vinegar

1. In a food processor, gently process the bell pepper, onion, carrot, and parsley, being careful not to overprocess (don't let mixture become mushy). Place in a large bowl. Cut up half the cabbage into chunks and place them in the food processor. Process lightly (once again, don't let the cabbage become mushy). Add to the other vegetables.
2. Thinly slice the remaining cabbage. Add to the bowl. In a separate bowl, mix the remaining ingredients and allow to stand for a few minutes. Pour over slaw ingredients and toss. Chill for at least an hour.

MONDAY, JUNE 2

TUESDAY, JUNE 3

Avoid the crowds—go shopping for
Father's Day and graduation gifts today

WEDNESDAY, JUNE 4

THURSDAY, JUNE 5

FRIDAY, JUNE 6

SATURDAY, JUNE 7

SUNDAY, JUNE 8

If I could choose the perfect day for a boating picnic, it would be Father's Day (which I always loved celebrating with my daddy, just like in this picture). A boating picnic is one of my favorite things to do— nothing stimulates your appetite like the water, and there ain't nothing better than food on a boat. Michael has lived his whole life in one place—the spot where we built our house. He loves the water so much he had to figure out how to make a living on it, so he became a harbor pilot, the guy who gets on ships in the ocean channel and navigates them to the docks. For our Father's Day celebration, it's only natural that we would wind up on a boat with picnic baskets filled with delicious food!

MONDAY, JUNE 9

TUESDAY, JUNE 10

Make that list of graduates you want to
congratulate, from nursery school all the
way up to grad school

WEDNESDAY, JUNE 11

THURSDAY, JUNE 12

FRIDAY, JUNE 13

Cover up your head and stay in bed!

SATURDAY, JUNE 14

Flag Day

SUNDAY, JUNE 15

Father's Day

In Albany, Georgia, where I was raised, high school graduations were such a big, big deal. Friends and relatives would throw parties for the graduates, their friends, and family, and we would go to one party after another. One of my favorite parties ever was the one my Aunt Peggy threw for me. It was a Coca-Cola party! Aunt Peggy and Uncle George had a beautiful yard with a birdbath in the garden; Aunt Peggy filled the birdbath with ice and had six-inch bottles of Coke standing up in the ice. My friends and I stood around and talked and gossiped and laughed. No matter how old you get, just remember: Graduations are a time to celebrate. You have proven that you have staying power!

MONDAY, JUNE 16

TUESDAY, JUNE 17

WEDNESDAY, JUNE 18

THURSDAY, JUNE 19

The Bag Lady opened in 1989

FRIDAY, JUNE 20

Summer officially begins

SATURDAY, JUNE 21

SUNDAY, JUNE 22

Celebrate all graduates!

Hummingbird Cake

Although my special Birthday Sunday rule involves buying each celebrant a personalized store-bought cake as well as making one cake from scratch, there are some times that just call for going all out. But going all out doesn't necessarily mean making something that is difficult. The following show-stopper may look like a challenge, but it is deceptively simple—and mouth-wateringly delicious. This old favorite is so easy—you just dump all of the ingredients into a bowl and stir!

Serves 12

CAKE

3 cups self-rising flour
2 cups granulated sugar
³/₄ cup vegetable oil
¹/₂ cup finely chopped pecans
2 very ripe large bananas, mashed
One 8-ounce can crushed pineapple,
    with juice
1 teaspoon vanilla extract
1 teaspoon ground cinnamon
4 large eggs, beaten

ICING

One 1-pound box confectioners' sugar
One 8-ounce package cream cheese,
    at room temperature
6 tablespoons (³/₄ stick) butter,
    softened
1 teaspoon vanilla extract
1 tablespoon milk, or more if needed
¹/₂ cup finely chopped pecans

1. Preheat the oven to 325°F.
2. Grease and flour three 8-inch round cake pans. In a large mixing bowl, combine the flour, sugar, oil, pecans, bananas, pineapple, vanilla, cinnamon, and eggs. Stir well with a spoon until the batter is smooth.
3. Pour the batter into the prepared pans. Bake for 26 to 28 minutes, until the tops spring back. Cool in the pans for about 10 minutes, then loosen from the pans and invert onto wire racks to cool completely.

4. To make the icing, mix the sugar, cream cheese, butter, vanilla, and 1 tablespoon milk in a large mixing bowl with an electric mixer until smooth. If needed, add more milk, 1 teaspoon at a time, to achieve the proper consistency. Ice between the cake layers, and on the sides and top of the cake. Sprinkle the top with the pecans. Refrigerate until ready to serve.

MONDAY, JUNE 23

TUESDAY, JUNE 24

WEDNESDAY, JUNE 25

THURSDAY, JUNE 26

FRIDAY, JUNE 27

SATURDAY, JUNE 28

SUNDAY, JUNE 29

Birthday Sunday!
My son Jamie's birthday!

The Fourth of July just has to be spent outdoors. I am lucky enough to live in a perfect spot for outdoor celebrating—my house sits right on a creek. I just love it when all of my family gathers, and the dogs are running around, and everyone—including the dogs—cools off in the creek. Low-Country Boil is probably the number one favorite at our house for summer entertaining, July Fourth included. Everything that's fresh—shrimp, maybe some crab legs or blue crab if Bobby's caught some, sausage— goes into the pot, then you just throw it all out on the table and everybody gets to diggin' in. After we're all cooled off in the creek, we have a flag cake or a big ol' slice of mud pie. So raise your flag and get to celebrating this great day!

Sunday	Monday	Tuesday	Wednesday	Thursday	Friday	Saturday
		1	2	3	4	5
6	7	8	9	10	11	12
13	14	15	16	17	18	19
20	21	22	23	24	25	26
27	28	29	30	31		

July

Low-Country Boil

Low-Country Boil is more of a technique than a recipe, and I'm about to tell ya just how to do it so that you have the best dish you could ever hope for. You have to start with quality ingredients, and you have to follow the directions exactly to have them all cooked perfectly.

¼ pound fully cooked smoked sausage per person, cut into 1-inch pieces
¼ cup Old Bay seasoning, or more to taste
2 small new potatoes per person
1 ear fresh corn per person, shucked, silked, and broken in half

½ pound large fresh shrimp per person (16-to-20-count size), shell on
Tartar sauce
Cocktail sauce
Potato sauce

Fill a large pot with enough water to cover all the ingredients. Add the sausage and Old Bay seasoning and allow to boil for about 20 minutes so that the sausage can flavor the water. Taste, and add more Old Bay if you think you need it. Add the potatoes and boil for about 15 minutes. Add the corn and boil for about 10 minutes more. Finally, add the shrimp and allow to cook for 3 minutes. Taste a shrimp and if it is cooked through, drain immediately and serve on an oversize platter or, as we do, on a table covered with newspaper! Serve with the three sauces, which are available in supermarkets or can be made using recipes in my book *Paula Deen Celebrates!*

MONDAY, JUNE 30

TUESDAY, JULY 1

My daughter-in-law Brooke's birthday!

WEDNESDAY, JULY 2

Get out the red, white, and blue napkins
and plates, and get ready to party!

THURSDAY, JULY 3

The dog days of summer begin

FRIDAY, JULY 4

It's the nation's birthday!

Independence Day

SATURDAY, JULY 5

SUNDAY, JULY 6

The Lady's Bouillabaisse

You'll find a very strong French influence in the South, especially in places like New Orleans and coastal Georgia, where the food can have a very clear southern Gallic twist to it, because of the freshness of the seafood. Bouillabaisse is a specialty of the South of France, but if you're living or visiting on the coast of Georgia, you're bound to see it offered on menus there as well. Feel free to add any of your favorite shellfish to the pot.

Serves 8

2 pounds mussels
2 pounds firm fresh fillets, such as
    grouper or striped bass
3/4 cup olive oil
1 1/2 tablespoons finely chopped garlic
1 1/2 cups chopped onions
5 Roma tomatoes, peeled and sliced, or
    2 cups canned Italian tomatoes
2 teaspoons fennel seeds

1/4 teaspoon saffron
1 tablespoon plus 1/2 teaspoon kosher
    salt
1 1/2 teaspoons freshly ground pepper
One 8-ounce bottle clam juice
4 whole crabs, cut in half
1 pound unpeeled raw shrimp
1 loaf French bread
Butter

1. Scrub and debeard the mussels in cold water. In a large, heavy pot, bring 2 cups of water to a boil. Add the mussels and cover the pot. Steam for 6 to 8 minutes, or until the mussels open. Discard any mussels that didn't open. Remove from the heat and set aside. Cut the fish into 1-inch thick slices.

2. Heat the oil in a large pot. Add the garlic, onions, tomatoes, fennel seeds, saffron, salt, and pepper. Add 5 cups of boiling water and the clam juice. Bring to a rolling boil, add the crabs and fish, and continue to boil for 6 to 8 minutes. Add the mussels and their broth to the pot along with the shrimp, and boil for an additional 5 minutes.

3. Slice the French bread, butter it, and toast lightly. Serve the bouillabaisse in large individual bowls lined with the toasted bread; pile in the seafood and ladle the broth over it. Top each bowl with 1 tablespoon of butter. Pass the remaining bread at the table.

Tip: When boiling any shellfish, add 1 teaspoon of vinegar to the water. This helps to loosen the meat from the shell.

MONDAY, JULY 7

TUESDAY, JULY 8

WEDNESDAY, JULY 9

THURSDAY, JULY 10

FRIDAY, JULY 11

SATURDAY, JULY 12

Take the pooches for a swim!

SUNDAY, JULY 13

Celebrate Bastille Day (a day early!)
with a pot of The Lady's Bouillabaisse!

There's nothing quite like an extended family vacation. You know, not just an extended vacation, but one with all the extended family—aunts and uncles and cousins and grandparents! We know the old saying about family and fish—don't keep either longer than three days, 'cause after that they both  *start to stink. But some of my own best memories come from vacations with relatives—fishing, crabbing, playing horseshoes, volleyball, cards, Pictionary, Clue, or poker. Food always plays a big part in these memories, and I've learned how to cook for a crowd without sacrificing my own relaxin' time! Here are a few of my favorite extended-family-vacation tips:*

    * *Do as much of the cooking as you can before the vacation, or it's no vacation at all. Ask family members for their favorite casserole recipes, which can be doubled or tripled and frozen ahead of time.*

    * *Take along some boxed mixes to make corn or blueberry muffins, or buy frozen biscuits or yeast rolls. Come on, girls, you're on vacation, not competing in the Pillsbury Bake-Off!*

    * *Divide the cooking responsibilities among the families who will be vacationing, with each family taking a night to cook. This means you'll always have a variety of cooking styles, and no one person will have to do all the work.*

MONDAY, JULY 14

Bastille Day

TUESDAY, JULY 15

WEDNESDAY, JULY 16

Is it possible that July is half over?

THURSDAY, JULY 17

Pick some fresh flowers—I'd choose the
hummingbird clethra, which, in Georgia,
blossoms beautifully in mid-July

FRIDAY, JULY 18

SATURDAY, JULY 19

SUNDAY, JULY 20

Birthday Sunday!

Vanilla Bean Custard Ice Cream

My friend David Slagel created this recipe for a potluck picnic; he and others churned many quarts of ice cream for the occasion, but this received the highest accolades, and is a sinfully good way to celebrate National Vanilla Ice Cream Day!

Makes about eight ½-cup servings

1½ cups whole milk
1½ cups whipping cream
1 vanilla bean, split in half lengthwise

3 egg yolks
⁷⁄₈ cup sugar
Pinch of salt

1. Combine the milk and cream in the top of a double boiler. Scrape the soft seeds from the vanilla bean and add half the seeds and half the pod to the pot. Heat the milk mixture over simmering water until it is hot and steaming, stirring constantly to prevent scorching, for 15 minutes. Let cool, uncovered, for 15 minutes.

2. Beat the egg yolks, sugar, and salt with an electric mixer until fluffy and a light yellow color, about 3 minutes.

3. Strain the cooled milk mixture into the egg mixture, and mix at a low speed until combined, about 2 minutes. Return the mixture to the double boiler and cook over medium low heat for 10 to 15 minutes, until thick enough to coat the back of a spoon. Strain into a container with a tightfitting lid. Cool overnight in the refrigerator or in an ice bath.

4. Pour the cooled mixture into an ice cream maker and freeze according to the manufacturer's instructions.

MONDAY, JULY 21

TUESDAY, JULY 22

WEDNESDAY, JULY 23
National Vanilla Ice Cream Day!

THURSDAY, JULY 24

FRIDAY, JULY 25

SATURDAY, JULY 26

SUNDAY, JULY 27

When August rolls around, it's always hard to believe that summer is almost over. Before you know it, the kids will be heading back to school, the Georgia Bulldogs will launch another football season, and everyone's schedules will start to fill up with parties and sporting events and the like. But the fun's not over yet. I really like to savor those lazy days in August by inviting friends over, heading out to the deck or the backyard, and making sure that everyone brings a fresh, simple dish so that none of us has to work too hard!

Sunday	Monday	Tuesday	Wednesday	Thursday	Friday	Saturday
					1	2
3	4	5	6	7	8	9
10	11	12	13	14	15	16
17	18	19	20	21	22	23
24	25	26	27	28	29	30
31						

August

Sweet Tea

I'm not big on alcohol, and neither is my good friend Martha Nesbit. But we know a good punch when we taste it! Sweet tea is my personal favorite non-alcoholic drink, and you'd be hard-pressed to find a real Southerner who doesn't love it! The hotter the weather gets, the sweeter we want our tea! I like mine with fresh mint.

Makes 2 quarts, about 10 servings

7 tea bags
1 cup sugar

Mint sprigs
Lemon wedges

Bring 4 cups of water to a boil in a kettle. Add the tea bags and turn off the heat immediately. Place the lid on the kettle and allow the tea to steep for 1 hour. Remove the tea bags and pour the tea into a pitcher. Add the sugar and stir to dissolve. Add 4 cups of cold water. Serve over ice with a sprig of mint and a lemon wedge.

Tip: You can make sweet tea with any kind of tea—herbal, caffeinated, or decaffeinated—and it will still be absolutely delicious.

MONDAY, JULY 28

TUESDAY, JULY 29

WEDNESDAY, JULY 30

Aunt Peggy's birthday!

THURSDAY, JULY 31

FRIDAY, AUGUST 1

SATURDAY, AUGUST 2

SUNDAY, AUGUST 3

Peach Cream Tart

If you've never had a good Georgia peach, I urge you to try one, especially during National Peach Month. You'll be amazed at its juiciness and flavor! This tart is so pretty and good. Make it a couple of hours before your party, and leave it at room temperature. The crust is like a shortbread cookie; you don't have to roll it out, and it doesn't get soggy.

Serves 6

CRUST
1 1/4 cups all-purpose flour
1/2 cup (1 stick) butter, softened
2 tablespoons sour cream

GLAZE
1/2 cup peach preserves or jelly
1 tablespoon frozen lemonade
    concentrate

FILLING
About 6 medium peaches, peeled and
    thickly sliced, or one 28-ounce can
    and one 16-ounce can sliced peaches
    in light syrup, well drained
3 large egg yolks
3/4 cup sour cream
3/4 cup sugar
1/4 cup all-purpose flour

1. Preheat the oven to 375°F.

2. To make the crust: Place the flour, butter, and sour cream in a food processor, and pulse to combine. When the dough has formed a ball, pat with lightly floured hands into the bottom and sides of an ungreased 10-inch tart pan with a removable bottom and ½-inch sides, or a round au gratin dish. Bake for about 15 minutes, until the crust is set but not browned. Let cool while preparing the filling. Lower the oven temperature to 350°F.

3. To make the filling: Arrange the peach slices in overlapping circles on top of the crust, until it's completely covered. Overfill the crust, as peaches will draw up during cooking.

4. Combine the egg yolks, sour cream, sugar, and flour, and beat until smooth. Pour the mixture over the peaches. Place the tart pan on a baking sheet and bake for about 1 hour, until the custard sets and is pale golden in color. Cover with an aluminum foil tent if the crust gets too dark. Transfer the tart pan to a wire rack to cool. When cool, remove the side wall of the pan.

5. To make the glaze: Combine the preserves or jelly and lemonade. Spread with a pastry brush over the top of the warm tart. Serve the tart warm, at room temperature, or chilled.

MONDAY, AUGUST 4

TUESDAY, AUGUST 5

Celebrate National Peach Month

WEDNESDAY, AUGUST 6

THURSDAY, AUGUST 7

FRIDAY, AUGUST 8

SATURDAY, AUGUST 9

SUNDAY, AUGUST 10

Everyone knows how I feel about my boys, Jamie and Bobby, and now my little baby grandson, Jack. I have been so blessed to also gain two more family members, Anthony Michael and Michelle Groover, Michael's children, and so my brood just seems to get bigger and bigger with every passing year. I'm always proud of my boys, but I especially like to think about all of their accomplishments during August, which is National Sons and Daughters Month. They truly have been with me every step of the way. When I started my catering company, The Bag Lady, it was Jamie and Bobby delivering meals to people in their offices all day long. And when we opened our first restaurant, they worked almost as hard as I did—Bobby as a dishwasher and baker and Jamie as a line cook. They've sacrificed so much to get us where we are today, and I feel so blessed to be their mother. After all, my restaurant isn't called The Lady & Sons for nothing!

MONDAY, AUGUST 11

National Sons and Daughters Day:
I'm going to celebrate with all my kids!

TUESDAY, AUGUST 12

WEDNESDAY, AUGUST 13

THURSDAY, AUGUST 14

Time to shop for school supplies

FRIDAY, AUGUST 15

SATURDAY, AUGUST 16

SUNDAY, AUGUST 17

Chocolate Chewy Cookies

This week in August marks the birthday of my first grandson, Jack Deen. I can't wait until he gets old enough to help me make these wonderful cookies! Naturally, most kids just love cookies and chocolate, and I expect that Jack will be no different. These cookies are best eaten within twenty-four hours, which is usually not a problem.

Makes 18 big cookies

2 cups confectioners' sugar, sifted
2 tablespoons cocoa, sifted
¼ teaspoon salt

⅓ cup all-purpose flour, sifted
3 egg whites
1 cup chopped pecans, toasted

1. Preheat the oven to 350°F. Line two baking sheets with parchment paper. Stir together the sugar, cocoa, salt, and flour. Add the egg whites one at a time. Beat well, then stir in the pecans. The batter will be very thin.

2. Drop by tablespoonfuls onto the prepared baking sheets. Bake for 12 to 15 minutes, until the cookies have begun to brown on the bottom and appear "set." Allow to sit for about 2 minutes undisturbed, then remove the cookies to wire racks to cool completely. Store in airtight containers.

MONDAY, AUGUST 18

TUESDAY, AUGUST 19

WEDNESDAY, AUGUST 20

THURSDAY, AUGUST 21

My baby grandson, Jack Deen, was born today!

FRIDAY, AUGUST 22

SATURDAY, AUGUST 23

SUNDAY, AUGUST 24

Birthday Sunday!

$\mathcal{L}$abor Day weekend is the perfect time to get out there and do some grilling. Gathering all your friends and family together to enjoy a big ol' brisket lovingly basted for hours over an open flame—well, that's just unbeatable in my book! But you don't have to limit yourself to barbecued beef (although I certainly could): Chicken, vegetables, shrimp, and especially salmon all work wonderfully well cooked on a grill. Over the years, we've decided that the flavor imparted by charcoal grilling is simply divine, but you just cannot beat the ease of a gas grill; it's so simple to control the temperature. Just turn it on, and you're good to grill!

MONDAY, AUGUST 25

TUESDAY, AUGUST 26
Send out casual, fun invites for Labor Day party

WEDNESDAY, AUGUST 27

THURSDAY, AUGUST 28
Take the kids back-to-school shopping

FRIDAY, AUGUST 29
Beginning of Labor Day weekend

SATURDAY, AUGUST 30

SUNDAY, AUGUST 31

*O*ur friends Alison and Danny Mahfet, of Savannah, are huge Dawg (as in Georgia Bulldawg) fans. Alison graduated from the University of Georgia in 1997, and her brother, Will Ronning, graduated in 1993. Years ago, Alison, Will, and some of their closest friends pooled their resources to buy a parking space (along with their season tickets) near the Georgia stadium, where, each home game, they set up an elaborate tailgate party. It is not unusual to find this kind of devotion in Georgia folks, and tailgating is by no means just limited to the state of Georgia—if you love football as much as we love our Dawgs, you'll find a way to throw a big ol' football party right out of the back of your car!

Sunday	Monday	Tuesday	Wednesday	Thursday	Friday	Saturday
	1	2	3	4	5	6
7	8	9	10	11	12	13
14	15	16	17	18	19	20
21	22	23	24	25	26	27
28	29	30				

September

Pimiento Cheese

There's always a huge fight if Alison forgets to make the pimiento cheese spread for our tailgate parties. Serve it on Wheat Thins or as a sandwich filling. Some people also use it to stuff celery sticks.

Makes 3 ½ cups

One 8-ounce package shredded sharp
    Cheddar cheese
One 8-ounce package shredded
    extra-sharp Cheddar cheese

One 4-ounce jar pimientos, with juice
¼ cup mayonnaise
Salt and pepper

Mix the shredded cheeses together with the pimientos and juice. Stir in the mayonnaise. With a metal spoon (pimientos will stain plastic or wood), stir until the mixture is well blended. Add salt and pepper to taste and stir again. Keep covered in the refrigerator until ready to use. It is easier to spread if left out on the counter for about 30 minutes before serving.

MONDAY, SEPTEMBER 1

National Rice Month starts!

Labor Day

TUESDAY, SEPTEMBER 2

WEDNESDAY, SEPTEMBER 3

THURSDAY, SEPTEMBER 4

FRIDAY, SEPTEMBER 5

SATURDAY, SEPTEMBER 6

Celebrate Georgia Bulldawg season by having a tailgate party

SUNDAY, SEPTEMBER 7

Green Beans with New Potatoes

The early fall always seems like a good time to make heftier foods—grilled corn on the cob, squash casseroles—and I like to reach back into my family recipe book to re-create for my children the comfort dishes that I remember so well. Jamie and Bobby's favorite green beans were cooked by their Great-grandmother Paul. She used very little water and always wilted them.

I serve these delicious green beans alongside corn bread and sliced tomatoes with onions. The fact that Michael loves them so much proves to me what a great teacher Grandmama Paul truly was.

Serves 8 to 10

3 pounds fresh green beans
¼ pound salt pork, sliced
¼ cup bacon grease (pour this into a
    jar and keep on hand in the
    refrigerator to use as needed)
2 cups chicken broth, plus more if
    needed (canned is fine)

2 to 3 teaspoons House Seasoning
    (recipe is at the end of this
    calendar)
12 small red potatoes, or more
1 onion, cut into slivers

1. Remove the ends from the beans. Snap the beans in two, place in a colander, wash, and set aside to drain.

2. Meanwhile, in a large cast-iron Dutch oven, lightly brown the salt pork in the bacon grease over medium heat, turning often, for approximately 10 minutes.

3. Toss the green beans into the pot, stirring them with a wooden spoon to coat well with the pork fat and bacon grease. Add the broth and the House Seasoning. Cook over medium-low heat, covered tightly, for approximately 30 minutes, or until the beans are done.

4. While the beans are cooking, peel a center strip from each new potato with a potato peeler. After 30 minutes, add the potatoes and onion to the beans; add ¼ cup more broth if needed. Cook, covered tightly, until the potatoes are tender, approximately 25 to 30 minutes, periodically checking the pot to make sure a small amount of liquid remains. When the potatoes are tender, tilt the lid slightly, off to the side of the pot, and continue to cook until the green beans are wilted, approximately 15 minutes.

Tip: For phenomenal beans, stir often. Add additional chicken broth in small amounts as needed, but don't drown your beans.

MONDAY, SEPTEMBER 8

TUESDAY, SEPTEMBER 9

WEDNESDAY, SEPTEMBER 10

THURSDAY, SEPTEMBER 11

FRIDAY, SEPTEMBER 12

SATURDAY, SEPTEMBER 13

Start your fall garden cleanup

SUNDAY, SEPTEMBER 14

*F*all is the perfect time to start getting back into your kitchen to cook up the foods that your family and friends just love. After a summer of being outside, this is the time to start thinking about getting cozy, and I have just the perfect tips to help you in your kitchen endeavors, whether you're baking or cooking:

* 1 1/2 cups corn syrup equals 1 cup sugar dissolved in 1/2 cup water.
* To remove excess grease from soups, drop a lettuce leaf in and watch it absorb the grease. Repeat until the desired amount is removed. Discard the lettuce.
* To keep unused egg yolks fresh for future use, place in a bowl and cover with 2 tablespoons of oil. They will remain fresh for 4 to 5 days.
* If you're out of tomato juice, substitute 1/2 cup tomato sauce mixed with 1/2 cup water for 1 cup of tomato juice.
* If you want to achieve a lighter texture in your baking, add a teaspoon of baking powder to any recipe calling for self-rising flour or self-rising cornmeal.
* Out of sweetened condensed milk? Make your own: Mix 6 cups whole milk with 4 1/2 cups sugar, 1 stick of butter, and 1 vanilla bean (or 1 tablespoon vanilla). Cook over medium heat, reducing the liquid, for 1 hour. Stir occasionally. Cool. Yields 4 1/2 cups.
* If you're watching your fat intake, try substituting low-fat cheese, mayonnaise, sour cream, et cetera, for the full-fat versions.
* Never throw away chicken stock; fresh vegetables, such as peas, butter beans, turnip greens, collards, and rutabagas, are wonderful cooked in it. Stock may also be frozen for later use in soups and sauces.
* No buttermilk? To make 1 cup buttermilk, add 1 teaspoon distilled white vinegar to 1 cup fresh milk; let sour for 5 minutes.
* Always beat eggs before adding sugar.

MONDAY, SEPTEMBER 15

TUESDAY, SEPTEMBER 16

WEDNESDAY, SEPTEMBER 17

THURSDAY, SEPTEMBER 18

Organize summer photos and make copies
for your friends and family

FRIDAY, SEPTEMBER 19

SATURDAY, SEPTEMBER 20

Celebrate Oktoberfest—roll out the barrel!

SUNDAY, SEPTEMBER 21

Sweet Noodle Kugel

The week before Rosh Hashanah, the Jewish New Year, is the perfect time to consider having a traditional Shabbat, or Friday-night, dinner. Shabbat dinner is often held in someone's home for family and guests from out of town, and it is an intimate way to greet one another and to welcome the Sabbath together. Our good friends Robbie Hollander and her husband, Sandy, a Savannah restaurateur, shared some of their wonderful Shabbat recipes with us. This is everybody's favorite.

Serves 12

1 pound wide egg noodles, cooked and
    drained
1 cup (2 sticks) butter, melted
1 pound cottage cheese
2 cups regular or reduced-fat (2% or
    4%) sour cream
1 teaspoon ground cinnamon

1 cup sugar
2 teaspoons vanilla extract
6 eggs, beaten
1/2 cup raisins (optional)
One 8-ounce can crushed pineapple,
    drained (optional)

1. Preheat the oven to 350°F. Grease a 13-by-9-inch baking dish.
2. Combine the warm noodles and butter in a large glass bowl. Add the cottage cheese, sour cream, cinnamon, sugar, and vanilla, and stir gently. Add the eggs and mix gently but thoroughly. Add the raisins and pineapple, if using. Pour into the prepared baking dish and bake for 1 hour.

Note: If your guests keep kosher, do not serve this dish with meat.

MONDAY, SEPTEMBER 22

Clean out the hall closet and buy some new
good-quality wooden hangers to prepare for jacket weather

TUESDAY, SEPTEMBER 23

WEDNESDAY, SEPTEMBER 24

THURSDAY, SEPTEMBER 25

FRIDAY, SEPTEMBER 26

SATURDAY, SEPTEMBER 27

SUNDAY, SEPTEMBER 28

Birthday Sunday!

$\mathcal{Y}$ou can't turn a corner in October without starting to see pumpkins absolutely everywhere! From grocery stores to patios to front stoops, these behemoth members of the squash family are as beautiful as they are tasty...that is, most of them. Personally, when Halloween rolls around, I say the scarier the better! Use the little "sugar" pumpkins for baking and eating, but save the big ones for the end of the month. Roll up your sleeves, throw on a witch's hat, and start carving the biggest, meanest, brightest jack-o'-lantern on the block!

Sunday	Monday	Tuesday	Wednesday	Thursday	Friday	Saturday
			1	2	3	4
5	6	7	8	9	10	11
12	13	14	15	16	17	18
19	20	21	22	23	24	25
26	27	28	29	30	31	

October

Maple-Grilled Salmon with Pineapple Salsa

There just ain't no better fish for grilling than salmon. Salmon's rich flavor and the smoke from the grill make for a delicious combination. This is almost better the next day, served cold in a salad. Yum!

1 salmon fillet (6 ounces) per person

*MARINADE (ENOUGH FOR
4 FILLETS)*
1 tablespoon maple syrup
1 tablespoon teriyaki sauce

1 tablespoon pineapple juice
1 teaspoon minced fresh ginger
1 clove garlic, crushed
*1 tablespoon Southern Comfort or
    other bourbon*

1. Place the salmon fillets in a resealable plastic bag. Combine the marinade ingredients in a glass bowl or measuring cup. Pour the marinade over the fillets, seal the bag, and refrigerate for at least 1 hour or overnight.
2. In a grill basket sprayed with vegetable-oil cooking spray, grill the salmon skin side down over hot coals. Do not turn! Watch for the fish to cook from the bottom up; it takes about 15 to 20 minutes. Serve with Pineapple Salsa.

Pineapple Salsa

This version of pineapple salsa is cooked and has a lightly pickled flavor that perfectly offsets the sweetness of the salmon.

Makes enough for 4 fillets

*1 medium ripe tomato, chopped into
    small cubes*
¼ cup chopped bell pepper
2 pickled jalapeño slices, finely chopped
*½ cup pineapple chunks, fresh or
    canned in juice or syrup*

1 teaspoon salt
1 tablespoon sugar
1 tablespoon white vinegar

Place all of the ingredients in a small saucepan. Simmer for about 5 minutes. Let cool. Cover with plastic wrap and refrigerate until ready to serve.

MONDAY, SEPTEMBER 29

Rosh Hashanah begins at sundown

TUESDAY, SEPTEMBER 30

WEDNESDAY, OCTOBER 1

Welcome the harvest season: Fill your home
with some beautiful fall squashes and pumpkins
for a splash of autumnal color

THURSDAY, OCTOBER 2

FRIDAY, OCTOBER 3

Start the little ones thinking about Halloween costumes

SATURDAY, OCTOBER 4

SUNDAY, OCTOBER 5

Sautéed Red-Skinned Apples

Fall is the time of year to take advantage of all the luscious varieties of apples that are now available, and to use them regularly in your kitchen. Not just for eating anymore, apples can be baked, sautéed, included as part of a savory meal, or puréed and folded into a cake. No matter how you slice them, be sure to enjoy them as the weather begins to cool. This is so easy and pretty on the plate next to a roast or golden glazed Cornish game hens. And it's delicious over ice cream, too!

Serves 4

*4 medium-sized, tart red-skinned
    apples (such as a Fuji)
6 tablespoons butter*

*½ cup sugar
1½ to 2 teaspoons ground cinnamon*

1. Wash the apples in cold water and pat dry. Cut them into quarters, and remove the cores. Slice each quarter lengthwise into 4 slices.
2. Melt the butter in a medium-sized frying pan over medium heat. Add the apples and sugar and mix well. Sprinkle the apple slices with the desired amount of cinnamon. Reduce the heat to medium low and continue cooking for 12 to 15 minutes, stirring frequently, until the apples have reached the desired degree of doneness. When the apples are done, the butter and sugar mixture will have become a delicious syrup.
3. Serve warm.

MONDAY, OCTOBER 6

TUESDAY, OCTOBER 7

WEDNESDAY, OCTOBER 8

Yom Kippur begins at sundown

THURSDAY, OCTOBER 9

FRIDAY, OCTOBER 10

SATURDAY, OCTOBER 11

SUNDAY, OCTOBER 12

You know, I think there's nothing that the men in my family like any better than watching football. Michael enjoys a good football game, but my sons, Jamie and Bobby, and my brother, Bubba, just adore it. In fact, Jamie and Bobby are such big Georgia football fans that Bobby wound up giving his brother a bulldog who is a great-grandson of Uga, the mascot of the University of Georgia team. His name is Champ and he is precious. But in our family, it's not only the football that's important, it's the food that goes with it. You can't watch a game and not have a cold beer and something good to eat. Some of my favorite football dishes are corn chowder, taco soup, chili-cheese corn muffins, teriyaki and buffalo chicken wings, celery with blue cheese dressing, and fried onion rings with chili sauce. You can find recipes for all of them in my cookbooks, or you can improvise and try your own twists.

MONDAY, OCTOBER 13

TUESDAY, OCTOBER 14

WEDNESDAY, OCTOBER 15

THURSDAY, OCTOBER 16

FRIDAY, OCTOBER 17

SATURDAY, OCTOBER 18

SUNDAY, OCTOBER 19

Birthday Sunday!

The Lady & Sons Beef Vegetable Soup

One of the joys of cool-weather dining is that the foods we eat tend to be heartier and more stick-to-the-ribs (especially if they include ribs!). When football season gears up, I suggest packing a stadium lunch, including wide-mouth thermoses filled with mouthwatering, soul-warming soup. Don't let the lengthy ingredient list scare you away. It's really not as bad as it looks. Even my brother, Bubba, can make it. On a cold winter's day, it will make your tongue want to slap your brains out.

Serves 2 or 3 dozen people

2 1/2 to 3 pounds beef short ribs or a 2 1/2- to-3 pound boneless chuck roast
2 tablespoons vegetable oil (if using chuck roast)
1 tablespoon dried Italian seasoning
3 tablespoons dried parsley
1 teaspoon garlic powder
1 tablespoon beef bouillon granules
1 tablespoon House Seasoning (recipe is at the end of this calendar)
1 tablespoon seasoned salt
2 bay leaves
1/2 teaspoon black pepper

1 teaspoon celery salt
1 tablespoon Worcestershire sauce
1 1/2 cups chopped onion
One 28-ounce can diced tomatoes
1 cup thinly sliced carrots
1 cup diced celery
1 cup sliced green beans, fresh or canned
1 cup frozen black-eyed peas
1 cup frozen butter beans
1 cup cut okra, fresh or frozen
1 cup corn kernels, fresh or canned
1 cup diced potatoes
1/2 cup uncooked elbow macaroni
2 teaspoons Accent (optional)

1. If using chuck roast, heat the oil in a large skillet over medium heat. Place the roast in the skillet and cook until browned on both sides, about 5 minutes per side. Remove the roast from the skillet and cut it into 1½-to-2-inch cubes; discard the fat. Place the beef cubes in a large stockpot. (If using short ribs, you can put them right in the pot with no preparation.) Add 4 quarts of cold water, the seasonings, the onion, and the tomatoes, and bring to a boil over high heat. Cover the pot, reduce the heat so that the liquid simmers, and cook for 1½ to 2 hours, or until the meat is very tender.

2. If using short ribs, remove them from the pot and cut the meat from the bones, discard the bones and fat, and return the meat to the pot. Add the vegetables, potatoes, and macaroni, and return the soup to a boil, stirring to distribute the ingredients. Reduce the heat and simmer for 45 minutes. Add Accent, if desired, and adjust the other seasonings to taste.

MONDAY, OCTOBER 20

TUESDAY, OCTOBER 21

WEDNESDAY, OCTOBER 22

THURSDAY, OCTOBER 23

FRIDAY, OCTOBER 24

Make a big pot of soup for the football game

SATURDAY, OCTOBER 25

SUNDAY, OCTOBER 26

*H*alloween is one of my favorite holidays because it gives me an excuse to do what I love to do every day: have a whole lot of fun! I do admit, though, that my favorite costume moment actually wasn't on Halloween. When I married Michael in 2004, Jamie and Bobby crashed my bridal shower dressed in bridesmaids' gowns—complete with makeup and everything! I have never laughed so hard in my life. As a mother, I don't think I've ever been prouder. Just to know that they had enough confidence to do something like that and were that comfortable in their own skin meant the world to me.

MONDAY, OCTOBER 27

TUESDAY, OCTOBER 28

WEDNESDAY, OCTOBER 29

THURSDAY, OCTOBER 30

FRIDAY, OCTOBER 31

Halloween

SATURDAY, NOVEMBER 1

SUNDAY, NOVEMBER 2

Daylight Savings Time ends

T just love Thanksgiving! The whole family gathers, but you don't have the pressure of gift giving, which to me is so very stressful. Thanksgiving's all about family, it's all about food, and it's all about being together. If you've got a small family and you don't want to go the turkey route, a roasted hen is wonderful, or a roasted chicken. Or to really downsize, go with a Cornish game hen. But no matter what the bird is, for it to be Thanksgiving, I've got to have gravy. I've got to have the dressing. I've got to have some kind of cake with pumpkin in it!

Sunday	Monday	Tuesday	Wednesday	Thursday	Friday	Saturday
						1
2	3	4	5	6	7	8
9	10	11	12	13	14	15
16	17	18	19	20	21	22
23	24	25	26	27	28	29
30						

November

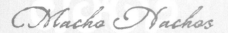
Macho Nachos

I don't make anything too strenuous during the weeks leading up to Turkey Day; I prefer simple dishes that leave me with the energy needed for wrestlin' with the turkey!

Very easy to put together, and absolutely delicious, this is a winner every time you serve it.

Serves 10

One 13.5-ounce bag white corn tortilla chips

One 16-ounce can refried beans, traditional, low-fat, or vegetarian

1 medium yellow onion, chopped

1 cup (¼ pound) shredded pepper jack cheese

1 fresh or pickled jalapeño pepper, seeds and veins removed, very finely sliced crosswise, plus extra for garnish

One 15-ounce can chili, with or without beans

1 cup (¼ pound) grated sharp Cheddar cheese

1 cup sour cream

½ cup chopped green onions

1 tomato, diced

1. Preheat the oven to 350°F.
2. On a large ovenproof platter, spread out a layer of tortilla chips. In a small saucepan over low heat, warm the refried beans until they are loose enough to spoon onto the chips. Put a teaspoon of beans on each chip. Working quickly, sprinkle the chips with onion, jack cheese, and jalapeño slices. Spoon on the chili and top with the Cheddar.
3. Place the platter in the oven and bake until the cheeses have melted, 5 to 10 minutes.
4. Remove from the oven and place on a trivet or heatproof surface. Top the nachos with the sour cream, green onions, diced tomato, and extra jalapeño slices, for garnish. Serve hot.

Tip: When working with jalapeños or other hot peppers, remember to wash your hands immediately after touching them, to remove dangerous oils.

MONDAY, NOVEMBER 3

TUESDAY, NOVEMBER 4

Election Day: Get out there and vote!

WEDNESDAY, NOVEMBER 5

THURSDAY, NOVEMBER 6

Countdown to Turkey Day

FRIDAY, NOVEMBER 7

SATURDAY, NOVEMBER 8

SUNDAY, NOVEMBER 9

In 2005, I tried something new on my television show: I made a turducken—a boneless turkey stuffed with a boneless duck stuffed with a boneless chicken, all tied together and baked with my famous corn bread dressing. You can order a turducken from the meat department in a large supermarket, or you may order a Cajun-style stuffed turducken from www.turducken.com. You should order several weeks in advance. Cooking instructions are included; be prepared to cook the turducken on a baking rack with a pan underneath for about 5 hours. When done, remove the turducken from the oven and place it on a carving board. (If you're planning to make brown gravy, you should add about 3 cups of water to the pan and use a wooden spoon to scrape up all of the drippings.) After removing it from the oven, allow it to cool about 15 minutes before carving. Slice thinly—there will be beautiful "ribbons" of the various meats.

One 15-pound turducken will serve about 20 people

MONDAY, NOVEMBER 10

TUESDAY, NOVEMBER 11

Veterans Day

WEDNESDAY, NOVEMBER 12

THURSDAY, NOVEMBER 13

FRIDAY, NOVEMBER 14

SATURDAY, NOVEMBER 15

SUNDAY, NOVEMBER 16

Birthday Sunday!

Southern Corn Bread Dressing

Northerners call their dressing stuffing, and Southerners call their stuffing dressing, but whatever you call it, it is, hands down, everyone's favorite Thanksgiving side dish. I like to make my dressing a little bit in advance, to let all the flavors meld together. This recipe is for a classic Southern soft dressing.

Serves about 20

CORN BREAD

2 tablespoons bacon grease or
    vegetable oil
1 cup self-rising cornmeal
1/2 cup self-rising flour
3/4 cup buttermilk
2 eggs

DRESSING

1 recipe Corn Bread, crumbled
4 slices white bread, dried in the oven
    and crumbled
40 (1 sleeve) saltine crackers, crumbled
1/2 cup (1 stick) butter
2 cups chopped celery
1 large yellow onion, chopped
1 teaspoon salt
1/2 teaspoon pepper
2 teaspoons poultry seasoning
7 cups chicken stock
5 large eggs, beaten

1. Preheat the oven to 400°F. Grease an 8-inch square or round metal pan with the bacon grease or vegetable oil.

2. Combine the cornmeal, flour, buttermilk, and eggs in a 1-quart bowl and mix well with a metal spoon. Pour into the prepared pan and bake for about 20 minutes, until very lightly browned on the top. Remove from the oven and allow to cool in the pan until cool enough to handle. Crumble.

3. In a large bowl, combine the crumbled corn bread, white bread, and saltine crackers. In a 12-inch skillet, melt the butter over low heat. Add the celery and onion and sauté until soft, about 10 minutes. Pour the sautéed vegetables over the corn bread mixture. Add the salt, pepper, and poultry seasoning.

4. About 1½ hours before you want to serve your meal, preheat the oven to 350°F. Spray a 13-by-9-inch baking dish with vegetable-oil cooking spray.

5. Add the stock to the corn bread mixture. Stir in the eggs. The mixture will be very soupy. Pour the mixture into the prepared dish. Bake the dressing for 50 minutes, until puffed and lightly browned. Serve with turducken and brown gravy.

MONDAY, NOVEMBER 17

TUESDAY, NOVEMBER 18

WEDNESDAY, NOVEMBER 19

THURSDAY, NOVEMBER 20

FRIDAY, NOVEMBER 21

SATURDAY, NOVEMBER 22

SUNDAY, NOVEMBER 23

Turkey and Stuffing Casserole

When you finish your meal, get one of your kitchen helpers to slice the turkey so that you'll have plenty of meat for sandwiches for the weekend. Cube and freeze what's left so that you can make this casserole sometime when you need something quick and easy. It won't win any James Beard Awards, but it will give your turkey a fresh look.

Serves 8

4 to 5 cups diced leftover turkey
One 10.75-ounce can condensed cream-
    of-mushroom soup
One 8-ounce container sour cream
3 cups herb-flavored stuffing mix
    (I like Pepperidge Farm)

$^{1}/_{2}$ cup (1 stick) butter, melted
1 cup chicken broth (canned is fine)

1. Preheat the oven to 350°F. Spray a 13-by-9-inch glass casserole dish with vegetable-oil cooking spray.
2. In a medium-sized bowl, stir together the turkey, soup, and sour cream. Place the mixture in the prepared dish and pat down evenly with the back of a spoon.
3. In a clean medium-sized bowl, stir together the stuffing mix, butter, and broth. Spread evenly over the turkey mixture.
4. Bake for 30 to 40 minutes, until the stuffing topping is browned and the casserole is hot and bubbly.

MONDAY, NOVEMBER 24

TUESDAY, NOVEMBER 25

WEDNESDAY, NOVEMBER 26

THURSDAY, NOVEMBER 27

Thanksgiving Day

FRIDAY, NOVEMBER 28

SATURDAY, NOVEMBER 29

SUNDAY, NOVEMBER 30

My family and I just love Christmas. It's all about family, food, and fun to us. Now that we have my little grandson, Jack Deen, running around, it's even more fun! I don't do a lot of variations on my Christmas Day meal. At my house, we are full up with turkey and ham from Thanksgiving, and at the restaurant, we have to cook so many turkeys and hams for Thanksgiving, and throw so many parties with turkey and dressing, that I am just sick to death of turkey by the time Christmas rolls around. All I want is beef. My favorite is a standing rib roast, but let me tell you something: I won't throw away a beef tenderloin, either. And naturally, you have to have a tater—a tater's got to be invited to the table in some shape, form, or fashion.

Sunday	Monday	Tuesday	Wednesday	Thursday	Friday	Saturday
	1	2	3	4	5	6
7	8	9	10	11	12	13
14	15	16	17	18	19	20
21	22	23	24	25	26	27
28	29	30	31			

December

You know, sometimes you really don't realize what an impression a homemade gift makes on somebody. Jamie told me one day, "Mama, do you remember when at Christmas-time, you'd go out and buy those little glass jars and you'd fill 'em with your homemade candy and put a ribbon on 'em and that would be my gift to my teachers? I would be so proud. I remember my chest puffing out when the teacher would say, 'Jamie, thank you so much. That was the most wonderful candy I've ever eaten.' Mama," he said, "you will never, never know how proud those homemade candies made me feel."

When you don't have much money, a simple gift of food delivered in a brown paper bag that you have sponge-painted with a Christmas tree or holly leaf can send such a personal message of sharing and caring. Here are some other ideas for homemade gifts. You can find all the recipes in my book Paula Deen Celebrates!

* *Fruited Rice Curry Mix*
* *Lemon-Dill Rice Mix*
* *Russian Spiced Tea Mix*
* *Greek Salad Dressing*
* *Peppermint Bark*
* *Pretzel-Peanut Bark*

* *Cheese Straws*
* *Oven Caramel Corn*
* *Icebox Fruitcake*
* *Orange-Ginger Butter*
* *Cinnamon-Honey Butter*
* *Herb Butter*

MONDAY, DECEMBER 1

Countdown to Christmas! Start making those homemade Christmas gifts!

TUESDAY, DECEMBER 2

WEDNESDAY, DECEMBER 3

If you haven't started your shopping yet, don't wait any longer!

THURSDAY, DECEMBER 4

FRIDAY, DECEMBER 5

SATURDAY, DECEMBER 6

SUNDAY, DECEMBER 7

National Pearl Harbor Remembrance Day

Before my brand-new grandson, Jack, came along, the most exciting Christmas was in 2005, when my niece, Corrie Hiers, helped me select the perfect gift to give her daddy, my brother, Bubba Hiers. Bubba wanted a dog, and I was able to find a chocolate Lab puppy in Atlanta. We met the people halfway, picked up the puppy, and managed to hide him from Bubba until Christmas morning. I put a note on his collar that said, "Hi, I'm not sure what my name is, but I know my daddy's name is Bubba. Would you please help me find him?" You couldn't slap the grin off Bubba's face all day long. Well, he named his puppy UB, after Uncle Bubba's, and UB is now Uncle Bubba's very best friend. Do you know how exciting it is to give somebody a gift that they want so badly?

MONDAY, DECEMBER 8

TUESDAY, DECEMBER 9

WEDNESDAY, DECEMBER 10

The Grand Ole Opry first broadcast today in 1927

THURSDAY, DECEMBER 11

Put up Christmas decorations

FRIDAY, DECEMBER 12

SATURDAY, DECEMBER 13

Michael's birthday!

SUNDAY, DECEMBER 14

Have a combination Birthday and
Sunday afternoon football party!

Cranberry Holiday Brie

This is one of those holiday dishes that is just beautiful to see. When you bring it to the table, the puff pastry is browned and beautiful, and then, when you slice into the cheese, the Brie oozes out and the cranberries peek through. The white on red makes it a perfect dish for the holidays—any occasion between Thanksgiving and Valentine's Day!

Serves 12

1 sheet (½ package) frozen puff
    pastry dough
1 egg
3/4 cup apricot preserves
2 tablespoons orange juice

¹/₃ cup dried cranberries
¹/₄ cup toasted sliced almonds
1 Brie cheese, about 13 ounces
Water crackers

1. Allow the pastry sheet to thaw in the package for about 30 minutes, until pliable. Preheat the oven to 400°F. In a small bowl, beat the egg with 1 teaspoon water to make an egg wash. Set aside.

2. Lightly flour a large wooden cutting board and roll out the pastry dough into a 14-inch square. Cut off the corners to make a circle. Save the extra dough to cut into decorative shapes for a garnish. Spread the apricot preserves on the pastry, leaving a 2-inch margin all around the edge.

3. Pour the orange juice into a small glass dish and add the cranberries, allowing them to absorb the flavor of the orange juice for about 5 minutes, until the cranberries are soft. Drain the cranberries. Arrange the cranberries evenly on top of the apricot preserves. Arrange the almonds evenly on the cranberries. Place the Brie on top of the almonds. Brush the edges of the puff pastry with the egg wash. Completely seal the Brie in the puff pastry. Seal the edges by brushing the egg wash on one edge, as if you are gluing the edges together.

4. Spray a baking sheet with vegetable-oil cooking spray. Place the Brie seam side down on the sheet. Decorate the top with pastry cutouts, rerolling scraps of dough, if desired. Brush the top with the remaining egg wash.

5. Bake for 20 minutes. Serve with crackers.

MONDAY, DECEMBER 15

TUESDAY, DECEMBER 16

WEDNESDAY, DECEMBER 17

THURSDAY, DECEMBER 18

FRIDAY, DECEMBER 19

SATURDAY, DECEMBER 20

SUNDAY, DECEMBER 21

Hanukkah begins at sundown

Standing Rib Roast

This recipe is one of my family's favorites. You can start it early in the day and finish it when it's time for dinner.

Serves 8 to 10

One 5-pound standing rib roast, bone in
1 tablespoon House Seasoning (recipe is
*   at the end of this calendar)*

1. Allow the roast to stand at room temperature for at least 1 hour. Preheat the oven to 375°F.
2. Rub the roast with House Seasoning. Place it on a rack in a roasting pan with the rib side down and the fatty side up. Roast for 1 hour. Turn off the heat and leave the roast in the oven; do not open the door.
3. About 1 hour and 10 minutes before serving time, turn the oven on to 375°F and reheat the roast for 30 to 40 minutes. Do not remove it or open the oven door from the time the roast is put in until the final roasting.
4. Remove the roast from the oven and tent with foil. Allow the meat to rest for 25 to 30 minutes before carving.

Tip: Allowing the meat to rest after roasting will result in a far juicier and more tender roast.

MONDAY, DECEMBER 22

First day of winter

TUESDAY, DECEMBER 23

WEDNESDAY, DECEMBER 24

Christmas Eve

THURSDAY, DECEMBER 25

Christmas Day

FRIDAY, DECEMBER 26

Boxing Day
First day of Kwanzaa

SATURDAY, DECEMBER 27

SUNDAY, DECEMBER 28

Crab and Spinach Casserole

Well, folks, it sure has been a busy year, and I'm looking forward to starting off 2009 with a bang! But New Year's Eve is probably my least favorite time to go out. What I really like is to spend the night at home—mine or someone else's. And rather than a heavy meal, I think hors d'oeuvres are nice for New Year's. This is a perfect New Year's Eve hors d'oeuvre if you love the combination of spinach and crabmeat, which I do.

Serves 8

Two 10-ounce packages frozen leaf
    spinach
1/2 cup (1 stick) butter
1 clove garlic, minced
2 tablespoons grated yellow onion
1/3 cup all-purpose flour
3 cups whole milk
1 cup (1/4 pound) grated Swiss cheese
1 cup half-and-half

2 teaspoons fresh lemon juice
Pinch of garlic powder
Dash of freshly grated nutmeg
1 teaspoon salt
1/4 teaspoon cayenne pepper
2 pounds fresh crabmeat, picked
    through twice for shells
1 cup fresh breadcrumbs

1. Preheat the broiler. Butter a shallow 2-quart baking dish or eight oven-proof individual ramekins or scallop shells.
2. Thaw the spinach in its packaging in the refrigerator overnight or defrost in the microwave following the package directions. Remove the packaging and squeeze the spinach to remove the water. Melt 2 tablespoons of the butter in a 12-inch skillet. Sauté the spinach with the garlic and onion over medium heat for 3 minutes. Transfer the spinach to the baking dish.
3. Melt 4 tablespoons of the butter in a 2-quart saucepan. Stir in the flour and whisk until smooth. Over low heat, gradually add the milk, stirring constantly with a spoon until smooth and thickened, 8 to 10 minutes. Add the cheese, half-and-half, lemon juice, garlic powder, nutmeg, salt, and cayenne. Cook over low heat until thickened again, about 10 minutes. Remove the sauce from the heat and carefully fold in the crabmeat.
4. Pour the mixture over the spinach. Sprinkle with the breadcrumbs and dot with the remaining 2 tablespoons butter. (You may need more breadcrumbs and butter if you're preparing individual ramekins.)
5. Broil about 5 minutes, until browned.

Tip: This dish can be prepared ahead and refrigerated covered. When ready to cook, preheat the oven to 350°F and bake for about 30 minutes, until bubbly. Change the oven setting to broil, and broil the top for about 5 minutes.

MONDAY, DECEMBER 29

TUESDAY, DECEMBER 30

WEDNESDAY, DECEMBER 31

What are you doing New Year's Eve?

THURSDAY, JANUARY 1

New Year's Day

FRIDAY, JANUARY 2

SATURDAY, JANUARY 3

SUNDAY, JANUARY 4

House Seasoning

1 cup salt
$^1/_4$ cup black pepper
$^1/_4$ cup garlic powder

Mix the ingredients well.
Store in a shaker near
the stove for convenience.

2007

JANUARY
	1	2	3	4	5	6
7	8	9	10	11	12	13
14	15	16	17	18	19	20
21	22	23	24	25	26	27
28	29	30	31			

FEBRUARY
				1	2	3
4	5	6	7	8	9	10
11	12	13	14	15	16	17
18	19	20	21	22	23	24
25	26	27	28			

MARCH
				1	2	3
4	5	6	7	8	9	10
11	12	13	14	15	16	17
18	19	20	21	22	23	24
25	26	27	28	29	30	31

APRIL
1	2	3	4	5	6	7
8	9	10	11	12	13	14
15	16	17	18	19	20	21
22	23	24	25	26	27	28
29	30					

MAY
	1	2	3	4	5	
6	7	8	9	10	11	12
13	14	15	16	17	18	19
20	21	22	23	24	25	26
27	28	29	30	31		

JUNE
					1	2
3	4	5	6	7	8	9
10	11	12	13	14	15	16
17	18	19	20	21	22	23
24	25	26	27	28	29	30

JULY
1	2	3	4	5	6	7
8	9	10	11	12	13	14
15	16	17	18	19	20	21
22	23	24	25	26	27	28
29	30	31				

AUGUST
			1	2	3	4
5	6	7	8	9	10	11
12	13	14	15	16	17	18
19	20	21	22	23	24	25
26	27	28	29	30	31	

SEPTEMBER
						1
2	3	4	5	6	7	8
9	10	11	12	13	14	15
16	17	18	19	20	21	22
23	24	25	26	27	28	29
30						

OCTOBER
1	2	3	4	5	6	
7	8	9	10	11	12	13
14	15	16	17	18	19	20
21	22	23	24	25	26	27
28	29	30	31			

NOVEMBER
				1	2	3
4	5	6	7	8	9	10
11	12	13	14	15	16	17
18	19	20	21	22	23	24
25	26	27	28	29	30	

DECEMBER
						1
2	3	4	5	6	7	8
9	10	11	12	13	14	15
16	17	18	19	20	21	22
23	24	25	26	27	28	29
30	31					

2009

JANUARY
				1	2	3
4	5	6	7	8	9	10
11	12	13	14	15	16	17
18	19	20	21	22	23	24
25	26	27	28	29	30	31

FEBRUARY
1	2	3	4	5	6	7
8	9	10	11	12	13	14
15	16	17	18	19	20	21
22	23	24	25	26	27	28

MARCH
1	2	3	4	5	6	7
8	9	10	11	12	13	14
15	16	17	18	19	20	21
22	23	24	25	26	27	28
29	30	31				

APRIL
			1	2	3	4
5	6	7	8	9	10	11
12	13	14	15	16	17	18
19	20	21	22	23	24	25
26	27	28	29	30		

MAY
					1	2
3	4	5	6	7	8	9
10	11	12	13	14	15	16
17	18	19	20	21	22	23
24	25	26	27	28	29	30
31						

JUNE
1	2	3	4	5	6	
7	8	9	10	11	12	13
14	15	16	17	18	19	20
21	22	23	24	25	26	27
28	29	30				

JULY
		1	2	3	4	
5	6	7	8	9	10	11
12	13	14	15	16	17	18
19	20	21	22	23	24	25
26	27	28	29	30	31	

AUGUST
						1
2	3	4	5	6	7	8
9	10	11	12	13	14	15
16	17	18	19	20	21	22
23	24	25	26	27	28	29
30	31					

SEPTEMBER
		1	2	3	4	5
6	7	8	9	10	11	12
13	14	15	16	17	18	19
20	21	22	23	24	25	26
27	28	29	30			

OCTOBER
				1	2	3
4	5	6	7	8	9	10
11	12	13	14	15	16	17
18	19	20	21	22	23	24
25	26	27	28	29	30	31

NOVEMBER
1	2	3	4	5	6	7
8	9	10	11	12	13	14
15	16	17	18	19	20	21
22	23	24	25	26	27	28
29	30					

DECEMBER
		1	2	3	4	5
6	7	8	9	10	11	12
13	14	15	16	17	18	19
20	21	22	23	24	25	26
27	28	29	30	31		

Year at a Glance

2008

JANUARY
		1	2	3	4	5
6	7	8	9	10	11	12
13	14	15	16	17	18	19
20	21	22	23	24	25	26
27	28	29	30	31		

FEBRUARY
					1	2
3	4	5	6	7	8	9
10	11	12	13	14	15	16
17	18	19	20	21	22	23
24	25	26	27	28	29	

MARCH
						1
2	3	4	5	6	7	8
9	10	11	12	13	14	15
16	17	18	19	20	21	22
23	24	25	26	27	28	29
30	31					

APRIL
		1	2	3	4	5
6	7	8	9	10	11	12
13	14	15	16	17	18	19
20	21	22	23	24	25	26
27	28	29	30			

MAY
				1	2	3
4	5	6	7	8	9	10
11	12	13	14	15	16	17
18	19	20	21	22	23	24
25	26	27	28	29	30	31

JUNE
1	2	3	4	5	6	7
8	9	10	11	12	13	14
15	16	17	18	19	20	21
22	23	24	25	26	27	28
29	30					

JULY
		1	2	3	4	5
6	7	8	9	10	11	12
13	14	15	16	17	18	19
20	21	22	23	24	25	26
27	28	29	30	31		

AUGUST
					1	2
3	4	5	6	7	8	9
10	11	12	13	14	15	16
17	18	19	20	21	22	23
24	25	26	27	28	29	30
31						

SEPTEMBER
	1	2	3	4	5	6
7	8	9	10	11	12	13
14	15	16	17	18	19	20
21	22	23	24	25	26	27
28	29	30				

OCTOBER
			1	2	3	4
5	6	7	8	9	10	11
12	13	14	15	16	17	18
19	20	21	22	23	24	25
26	27	28	29	30	31	

NOVEMBER
						1
2	3	4	5	6	7	8
9	10	11	12	13	14	15
16	17	18	19	20	21	22
23	24	25	26	27	28	29
30						

DECEMBER
	1	2	3	4	5	6
7	8	9	10	11	12	13
14	15	16	17	18	19	20
21	22	23	24	25	26	27
28	29	30	31			

Photograph Acknowledgments

JASON CLEVERING / THE WONDEERFUL GROUP:
cover image; title page; January month opener;
May, week 4; July, week 3; July, week 4;
August, week 5; November, week 2

ALAN RICHARDSON: January, week 4; February month opener;
February, week 1; March, week 3; March, week 4; April month
opener; April, week 3; May month opener; May, week 2; June month
opener; June, week 4; July month opener; August month opener;
September month opener; September, week 2; September, week 4;
October, week 3; December, week 1; December, week 4

MAC JAMIESON for *Cooking with Paula Deen* magazine:
February, week 3; August, week 4; October month opener;
November month opener; November, week 4;
December month opener; December, week 2

About the Author

PAULA DEEN is the bestselling author of *Paula Deen Celebrates!*, *Paula Deen & Friends: Living It Up, Southern Style; Paula Deen's Kitchen Classics;* and other books. She is the host of the Food Network's *Paula's Home Cooking* and *Paula's Party*, and has appeared on *Good Morning America, Today, Fox & Friends,* and *The Oprah Winfrey Show.* She lives with her family in Savannah, Georgia.

Y'all do not want to miss this!

Recipies • Entertaining Home Decor • Gardening Holiday Menus

Cooking with Paula Deen magazine shares the warmth of Paula's kitchen and her Southern hospitality, combining the love of delicious home-cooked meals with a lifestyle steeped in tradition. Each issue of *Cooking with Paula Deen* contains beautifully designed articles and recipes based on Paula's uncomplicated style of home cooking.

To order call 1-877-933-5736 or visit
www.pauladeenmagazine.com

Notes

Notes

Notes

Notes

Notes

Notes

Notes

Notes

Notes

Notes

Notes

Notes